A Plan
For The
Planet

One Way To Avoid
The "Tyranny Of The Majority"
In Our Democracies

BY

TED WELLS

Cover and title page font: Toulouse-Lautrec
Text fonts: Book Antigua, Arial, Arial Narrow, Times New Roman, Handwriting font: MICHAEL
Cover is a photograph of a 2005 village meeting in Siumu, Samoa by the Author. All other photos, diagrams and charts are by the Author.

ISBNs:
978-0-473-72747-5 (Hard Cover POD
978-0-473-72746-8 (Paperback POD)
978-0-473-72748-2 (Kindle)
978-0-473-72749-9 (PDF)

TO MY FAMILY AND FRIENDS
FOR THEIR WILLINGNESS
TO OVERLOOK MY OBSESSION
WITH CONSENSUS DECISION-MAKING,
PARTICULARLY WHEN I DON'T
ALWAYS PRACTICE IT MYSELF.

Acknowledgements

I would like to thank my wife, Helen Ann McLaren Wells, whose love, humor, intelligence and inspiration as my life's traveling companion for nearly 60 years has allowed me the time and space to put my ideas down on paper. I'd also like to thank my son, Tao McLaren Wells, whose creative thinking helped shape many of the ideas in this book, particularly those about the social blindness of capitalism and the many injustices inherent in our public institutions. Equally importantly, I'd like to thank my late son, Dr. Ian Cressy Wells, who showed me that life is not about the accumulation of wealth. It is about exploring, discovering and enjoying every day with family and friends.

There are many, many others who helped me clarify my thinking over the years. Some I've only known remotely through their work. Noam Chomsky has perhaps been the most influential, but there is also John Buck, the man who brought Sociocracy to the English speaking world. Others include Sharon Villines, Ted Rau, John Rohrbaugh, John Reuwer and, John Schinnerer who continue John Buck's work, and Edwin John who independently developed a very similar system of governance across many parts of India.

I am indebted to all of you and to everyone else I've met on my life's journey. You have been my good fortune.

In peace and with thanks

TED WELLS

NOTE: This booklet contains Chapters 1-10 & 16-19 of the Author's book: **Power, Chaos or Consensus?** 3rd Edition

It describes how the Plan For The Planet was developed, its overall structural and operating details, and how it might be implemented.

However, it does not discuss the many rights and responsibilities we will need to consider to resolve the global problems we now face. It also doesn't include the, very detailed Consocratic Plan itself. These are included in the full version of "Power, Chaos or Consensus?"

Table of Contents
A Plan For The Planet

One Way To Avoid
The "Tyranny Of The Majority"
In Our Democracies

Chapter 1: The Ethiopian Connection   7
Chapter 2: Is The Answer Really 42?   21
Chapter 3: Making Public Decisions
                    With Guns And Money   29
Chapter 4: Other Ways We Make
                    Public Decisions   39
Chapter 5: The Delphi Technique   51
Chapter 6: Lessons From The South Pacific   55
Chapter 7: The Key   69
Chapter 8: In Search of the "Big Picture   77
Chapter 9: So Where Should We Be Headed?   95
Chapter 10: The Complexity of Our Current Mess   105
Chapter 11: Personal Problems   (Not Included)
Chapter 12: Economic Problems   (Not Included)
Chapter 13: Equity Problems   (Not Included)
Chapter 14: Community Problems   (Not Included)
Chapter 15: Environmental Problems   (Not Included)
Chapter 16: The Principles and Structures
                    of a Consensus Based Democracy   113
Chapter 17: The Financial Implications   137
Chapter 18: Sociocracy
                    and Other Similar Paradigm   143
Chapter 19: A Way Out of This Mess   153
Chapter 20: The Consocratic Plan   (Not Included)
About the Author   171

Chapter 1:

The Ethiopian Connection *explains when and where the ideas about fixing the planet originated. It begins by explaining two observations made during the 3 years that my wife and I were volunteers helping a few dozen very poor, unschooled but very intelligent Amhara farmers clear jungle and start a new town in an extremely remote part of southern Ethiopia back in the late 1960s. The land had been personally given to them by the elderly, god-like Emperor, Haile Selassie, also an Amhara.*

Some pessimists among us think that the end of humanity is already written. They see the corrupting infuence of unfettered capitalism pushing our governments, our institutions and life as we know it, relentlessly toward a grimly obvious abyss. For them, the questions of catastrophic global warming, nuclear war and societal collapse are now about when, not if.

There are signs of this, of course. Who can ignore the extreme weather the planet is now experiencing, our new, seriously polarizing, narcissistic leaders like Putin and Trump still equating power with reason, and the ever mutating global pandemics that continue to threaten us all.

However, I'm not convinced that our looming demise is already cast in stone. I think it is realistically possible to peacefully reorganize our existing institutions, including our governments, one committee at a time, one community at a time, so that their inherent power and the avarice they sometimes generate no longer fuel their blind ambition and our own self-destruction.

This book is about one way it might happen. It originates from the experiences that I had more than 50 years ago while living in a grass hut in a very remote part of southwest Ethiopia. My wife and I had joined the American Peace Corps as an alternative to the Vietnam War and were given the opportunity to help several dozen Amhara highlanders clear a site for a new town in the dense lowland jungle of the Rift Valley. The land had been personally given to the villagers by the Emperor, Haile Selassie, also an Amhara. During the three years we were there, I was introduced to two fundamental principles of life:

1.   That essentially all people on this planet are alike, and
2.   That beyond this generality, all people on this planet are totally, absolutely and fundamentally different from one another.

The two are not mutually exclusive.

What I observed while living and working among people who had almost no material possessions or formal education was that despite this, they all had the same characteristics as the people with whom I grew up.

Even before witnessing the incredible poverty of Ethiopia I knew my childhood was privileged. I was born and raised in a small town in New England in an old banking family that could trace its ancestry back to the Mayflower. My family was full of intriguing characters and my classmates were a wonderful collection of personalities from comics to gods. I was sure my family and friends were unique on this planet.

Yet every group of Ethiopians I met seemed to contain similar proportions of those who were wise and intelligent and those who were mentally challenged; those who were kind and loving and those who liked hurting others; those who were content with what they had and those who lied, cheated and stole even from their friends; those who laughed all the time and those who never could see the bright side of anything.

8

Thankfully, the positive characteristics of people in any group far outweighed the negative. However, the familiar characteristics of the people I met in Ethiopia I have repeatedly observed since then while living, working and travelling as a professional Urban Designer and Planning Specialist in many other cultures and countries across the Americas, Europe, Asia, North Africa and the South Pacific.

Most, if not all of the characteristics of those I've met, seem to me to be traits that are actually part of our global genetic makeup not the construct of our variable environments. In that sense, I believe people around this planet are all much more alike than we might think.

However, Ethiopia also taught me on a more personal level, that however much one person or group of people might empathize with another, they can never fully understand them or think like them; that everyone's life experiences and mental makeup are so different that no two people ever think exactly alike about anything. The difference forced me to look at why I was in Ethiopia avoiding Vietnam on what I thought was a peaceful selfless mission to help others.

What I learned was that sometimes even peaceful selfless good intentions can have a serious downside to them, generating anger and hate between people rather than love and understanding. (See the companion publication of this book set in Ethiopia in the late 1960s called "The Old Man in the Bag and Other True Stories of Good Intentions", which chronicles some of the more subtle forms of power we encountered there.)

The full implications of my African experiences were not immediately obvious to me. When I returned to America and continued planning for the public good in institutions that appeared much more civilized than the ones I had encountered in Africa, I found myself very uncomfortable for some reason.

I soon figured out why. In rural Ethiopia, as poor and isolated as most people were, they all still remained in control of most of their own life choices. In the Western

9

world, almost half of every group, that is, everyone in the minority, have virtually no say at all over many significant aspects of theirs.

In the back woods of Ethiopia, there were no majority votes taken to make community decisions. There were no institutions telling them what they could and could not do. They did not base their decisions just on the financial costs of the choices they faced. They did not use questionnaires to find out what the majority thought and then make decisions that knowingly left out half of their group.

They intuitively recognized that despite their differences, whatever the cost, they needed the support of everyone, to live together in peace. They needed to reach consensus among themselves to survive.

The argument against using consensus decision-making in our own civilized institutions has always been the problem of scale. In modern societies there are just too many of us to be able to resort to such primitive, idealistic practices.

Democracies force us to turn all decisions into black and white choices even though life is not really like that. Democracies make decision-making easy by polarizing debate and creating winners and losers. Democratic decisions can sometimes get it right, but they can also create resentment and anger among those in the minority who lose out and a strong elation of success among the majority, when neither is deserved

What I learned from my experience in Africa was that such polarized responses are actually signs of paternalism between equals. Paternalism between father and son or teacher and student can generate love and understanding, but paternalism between two equals, when the only difference between them is wealth, power or respect, can generate anger and hate, or even violence, terrorism and war.

Back in late 1971, when I first began seriously thinking about minority rights and possible ways to overcome the downside of paternalism in our existing democratic institutions, I thought most of my ideas were new and unique. Through multiple attempts to write this book over nearly five decades, I have since found out that almost none of them are either new or unique.

Even back when I started, I knew from my childhood days singing in the church choir that I was not the first to think the world might be a better place if we treated everyone the same way we wanted to be treated ourselves. However, I did not know then that even Jesus wasn't the first person to think of this.

I also didn't know Hitler, who died in a Berlin bunker only a month before I was born and whose ideas in "Mein Kampf" consequently held a morbid fascination for me, wasn't the first to recognize the political power of prejudice. Somehow, too, I had always thought that Karl Marx, later indirectly supported by E.F. Schumacher, was the first to express serious reservations over the mindless, moral-less drive of the market place, but he wasn't.

When I started, I had not even heard of Mohammed's efforts to integrate political, social and economic behavior through his founding of Islam, nor of the Catholic priest, Arizmendiarrieta's more recent efforts to do the same through his founding of the Mondragon cooperatives in northern Spain.

11

In my university days, my heroes were the French political philosopher, Charles de Montesquieu, one of the brains behind the American Constitution and the Scottish Landscape Architect and urban design pioneer, Sir Patrick Geddes, one of the brains behind modern town planning.

I was fascinated with the ways they had each dispassionately tried to sort out the complex interrelationships between human institutions and their environment. I was a bit disappointed when I later read some of Confucius, Plato and Aristotle and found out that my two idols weren't quite the pioneers I had thought.

A number of relatively recent world celebrities from Albert Einstein to John F. Kennedy have pointed out that our current social and political institutions have not kept pace with our technological development, and I would agree . . . as I suspect would many people.

We have managed to go to the moon, and with the touch of a button can now destroy ourselves and every living thing on this planet. However, we have still not figured out how to ensure social equity between people under a market economy, how to live in the natural environment that surrounds us without abusing it, how to resolve serious conflicts with our neighbors without going to war.

§

Today, it is widely assumed that our present democratic or parliamentarian forms of government are the best we can hope for given the horrors of modern warfare and the relative benefits that these systems provide for the majority of people living under them. However, far from being at the end of political evolution, I am convinced our current democracies are only a partially developed ideology now in serious need of updating.

While better than most previous forms of government, our existing democracies still contain several potentially fatal flaws that make them inherently unstable and an impediment to us ever finding lasting peace on this planet. Among other things, democracies are presently incapable of equitably resolving minority grievances.

Even with the best of intention, in a democracy it only takes 51 percent of those involved in any decision to decide the fate of the other 49 percent. Within every democracy is the unquestioned assumption that the institutions of any majority group can fully understand and if necessary provide for the needs of any minority group, which is simply not true.

This serious shortcoming of democratic decision-making was foreseen but ultimately left unresolved 250 years ago by Adams, Madison, Mill, Tocqueville and others whose ideas helped form the US Consititution. Back then they called the problem "The Tyranny of the Majority." Today their worst fears have become a reality.

Our democracies have become a grim form of institutionalized paternalism that are neither a gift of the rich to the poor nor an obligation of the majority to the minority. They are now just an ignorant indulgence of power over the powerless and the inevitable generator of anger and hate.

Unfortunately, with the growth of technology, the decline of religion and the replacement of moral values with market place values, our majority based democracies are no longer capable of looking at all the major environmental and social issues we now face from any long term or global perspective.

Even more unfortunately, the more inclusive consensus decision-making method that might have overcome the "tyranny of the majority" has at least two serious drawbacks of its own. One is that it doesn't work in large groups, as I've already mentioned. A second is that in our current global mess any consensus based decision-making process can be easily hijacked by narcissistic participants.

However, just imagine if these problems with consensus could be resolved and this form of decision-making peacefully integrated into our current democratic forms of government? What a different world we might live in.

This, in fact, is the premise behind this book.

My belief that things could be improved on this planet might be because I am a die-hard planner. I was trained as an Architect, but I have spent most of my life helping local communities around the world plan their own futures. I suspect planning is part of my genetic makeup, although it could also be the result of the death of my father at an early age and my subsequent need to maintain control over my own environment.

Either way, I am not convinced that we have to go on living together the way we do now. I think with a bit of comprehensive planning, together we could solve, or at least seriously reduce, many of the global problems we now face without having to resort to violence, terrorism or war.

Comprehensive Planning is about influencing change peacefully to achieve a desired future that is not entirely obvious or certain. It is normally practiced on relatively small ideas at a local level, like running a business or improving the layout of a community, but it is capable of being used to solve much larger problems. Over the last 140 years, the practice of Planning has developed a simple almost self-evident 6-step method on how to achieve a better future.

1. Identify what the future state should be; that is, set the goals.
2. Identify and clarify the problems that may interfere with achieving these goals and the opportunities that may achieve them quicker or with fewer resources.
3. Identify and analyze (including side effects) alternative ways to solve the problems and utilize the opportunities to achieve the goals.
4. Choose the best way to do this; that is, come up with a "Plan".
5. Implement "The Plan".
6. Monitor subsequent change and if the results are not as expected, revise "The Plan" (or alternatively, modify the goals).

I have tried to follow these six steps as far as possible writing. "Power Chaos or Consensus?" It is my attempt to pull together the many personal experiences and observations I've had during a lifetime working on the edges of political decision-making preparing plans for all types of governments, NGO's and businesses around the world. Since choosing Ethiopia over Vietnam early in life I've wanted to find other peaceful ways to resolve the many problems we now face on this planet, ways that would:

- Enable many autonomous communities to live in the same area together peacefully,
- Remove power and the use or threat of force to resolve inter-community differences,
- Ensure gender equality in all political decisions,
- Ensure minorities are involved in all political decisions,
- Ensure social justice, environmental sustainability and economic rationality are always considered simultaneously when making any political decision,
- Ensure political representatives are personally known to those who select them,
- Ensure narcissists cannot buy their own selection as political representatives,
- Avoid election cycles which force short term solutions to long term problems,
- Remove social media manipulation and fake news from political decisions,
- Reduce the cost of government by ensuring the rapid, peaceful implementation of all political decisions..

The ideas contained in this book, I believe, would achieve these objectives and many others. I've called the ideas when considered collectively, "Consocratic Theory", and their political implementation, a "Consocracy". The term is simply the conjunction of two of its primary concepts; "consensus" and "democracy".

The first 10 chapters of my original book "Power, Chaos or Consensus?" are included in this book along with Chapters 16 through 18 of that book, which describe the principles and structural details of what an upgraded Democracy based on Consensus Decision-making might look like. Chapter 19 details the steps that people might take to see this plan introduced as an amendment to the constitutions of their own existing democracies.

Not included in this book are chapters 11 through 15 of my original book. These chapters describe over 50 major complex intertwined, global problems that I think all of humanity needs to sort out if we are to survive as a species. They are not included here because they could easily confuse the main reason for this book, which is to describe as simply as possible how a consensus based government might work.

Also not included in this book for the same reason is Chapter 20, the Consocratic Plan itself; namely the detailed goals, principles, rights, responsibilities and rules, which would establish a Consocracy and allow people to equitably govern themselves in peace and with social justice in both a market economy and a sustainable environment. Both of these omissions, however, can be found in my original full book "Power, Chaos or Consensus?".

§

I have not bothered to footnote all the politicians, planners, political scientists, philosophers, priests and members of the public whose thoughts have gone into writing either that book or this one. This is for two reasons.

First, neither book is a treatise written by someone steeped in academia. They are both one person's view of the world and its possible future, based on a lifetime involved in political decision-making. If any of the "facts" used to defend something here seem suspect, try Google or some other internet browser and see what a variety of other people think about them. It is an ever-growing wonder to me the range and depth of the well-documented thought that can be found there, if you take the time to sift through all the fake news and narcissism.

This probably sounds like a cop-out to those who really like footnotes, and I guess it is, but the second and much more important reason why there are no footnotes in either book is because there are no sources on this planet that can irrefutably prove (or disprove) the truth of anything I've written in them.

Unfortunately, I know all too well from the amount of time I have personally spent in court professionally defending (or destroying) the plans of others, that with enough money (or blind faith) it is possible to find a credible expert (or footnote) somewhere on this planet to support (or destroy) any point of view, however well reasoned (or implausible) it might be.

In today's complex world, if you have the time and money to look for them, you can always find more than one expert with a hot wax stamped Doctorate and an impenetrable ego who will stand up in court and say with perfectly sincere honesty and without a hint of doubt, that the earth is flat.

§

The "Consocratic Plan" described briefly in this book has come out looking something like a cross between the planning ordinances of a large city and the constitution of a small country. Such detail should not be surprising. Over the last few millennia, many others have tried to come up with idealized philosophies and religions on how we all might live together in peace, but all have been pretty vague on the details.

As a consequence, they have all been subjected to widespread misinterpretation and abuse. Some would even say their abuse has significantly contributed to our current global strife and disharmony rather than achieved what their original proponents had intended.

One of the more recent semi-detailed attempts to create a comprehensive system to manage human affairs was back in 1787 when members of the Constitutional Convention sat down in Philadelphia to draft the US Constitution.

What they came up with was brilliant for its day, and it has since been copied around the world many times. However, I believe it may be time to consider making some revisions to its general format given the substantially more crowded current state of our planet and the many wildly divergent, seriously complex and environmentally destructive market driven cultures that now inhabit it.

§

The plan described here, while reasonably detailed and precise is not fixed or final. One brain alone is not remotely enough to consider all the intimate ramifications of such a complex subject. Many more minds need to be brought to bear on the ideas presented here.

It might be wishful thinking, but what I hope happens sometime in the not too distant future is that other people will become motivated enough to further clarify the ideas set out here or come up with completely new ones. Through the internet, it would not take much to get many people involved in the process.

The website, www.consocracy.com has been established with the hope of setting up a global operating structure similar to that of Wikipedia at some point so that everyone will be able to contribute to its ultimate form and content.

It would not take much to try out the ideas I've described here, either. It would not require any law changes. All it would take is for a local committee or club in a small community somewhere to decide to make its decisions by consensus. It is something any of us could do, anywhere. It could simply be another step in the "think globally, act locally" approach to improving the world that has already been adopted by many socially and environmentally responsible people in many countries over the last few decades.

The use of consensus to make decisions in small groups has the remarkable effect of bringing people together rather than pulling them apart. Everyone knows how majority voting works, how it divides people, but consensus decision-making, now a lost art in most of the world, does exactly the opposite. It brings people together and it heals them. In time, once the benefits of using consensus to reach decisions in small groups are recognized, other parts of the system could be added gradually to manage narcissistic or paranoid participants and allow large groups to participate until a fully functioning Consocracy is up and running.

By that point, it is unlikely that it will look anything like what is described here. The Consocratic System is an almost "chaotic" structure. Its potential ability to spontaneously evolve as knowledge improves and reality changes, I think, could be one of its greatest assets.

With only moderate changes to existing institutions, however, I believe all people in a Consocracy would not only have control over what happens in their own homes among friends as most people have now, but have personal control over most of their own educational, medical, judicial, religious, environmental management, financial, and social support systems as well.

Though perhaps hard to comprehend at this point in time, the Consocratic System of governance would help resolve the serious intergenerational conflicts now found in Palestine, Israel, Syria, Turkey, Iraq, The Ukraine, Afghanistan, Ruanda, Thailand, Myanmar, Indonesia, and Tibet. It would stop the polarization of the people in the United States and other older democracies where the public interest has become subservient to corporate interests.

On a less dramatic scale, the festering problems of many indigenous people in colonized democracies, such as the native Indians of North America, the Aborigines of Australia, and the Maori of New Zealand would be substantially reduced if each were given real control over their own lives.

The value of the Consocratic System is that it is neither a religion nor a philosophy. It is simply a plan; a voluntarily imposed, collectively agreed, comprehensive, amendable, non-political set of civil laws that if adopted in accordance with local legal procedures could help any group of people peacefully evolve their existing social and political institutions from their current well intentioned, but inadequate forms, into institutions that would more closely meet the needs of all those affected by them.

I know such evolutionary improvements will not happen over night, but it would be nice to think that the love, trust, and social justice we human beings have managed to build among ourselves over the last few millennia despite our sometimes belligerent institutions, will not be forced from us altogether by their lingering inadequacies.

Chapter 2:

Is The Answer Really 42? *was written more than 30 years ago when I tried to clarify what I hoped to accomplish writing this book (which I had started two decades earlier). At the time, the New Zealand Government had almost gone bankrupt and I was only beginning to understand that the objectives of a successful market place, a just society and a sustainable environment have almost nothing in common with each other.*

I have been concerned about the planet's reliance on force to solve its problems since the Vietnam War, and had even tried to write about it back in the early 1970s, but up until the 1980s, despite some knowledge of Marx, I had not considered the market place as a significant contributor to the problem.

What changed this was New Zealand's desperate struggle to get through a very severe economic crisis during that decade. My wife and I along with our two small children had moved to New Zealand in 1977 after becoming disillusioned with American politics, in the hope of finding a better way of life. While we found a much more socially inclusive society in our new home, we also found a country struggling to survive economically.

In 1973, Great Britain had decided to join the Common Market and as a condition of entry, its new European trading partners had forced it to cut off almost all trade with New Zealand within ten years.

In the decades before this catastrophic event, New Zealanders had enjoyed one of the highest standards of living in the world (in some years, second only to Americans) largely because virtually everything it produced went directly to its colonial motherland.

Ten years after Britain joined the Common Market, however, New Zealand still had not found another major new trading partner, so it went into crisis mode. It radically slashed its social services and sold off most of its public assets including its national railway, national airline, national power system, national telephone service, national bank, national public works department and pretty much every other public asset it could lay its hands on. It even closed its national planning office where I was working at the time.

The Government needed the money and it was convinced by American economic thinking that private enterprise could run most things more efficiently anyway.

It was not long, however, before it was clear that many of the overseas corporate buyers only wanted to strip the remaining assets out of the former public facilities and services before bailing out and leaving them virtually bankrupt.

As a result, the country was eventually forced to buy some of them back, while the short-term owners walked away with their pockets full.

I was somewhat upset when it became obvious that foreign corporations were in New Zealand simply to make money out of the Country's misfortune, but I was much more upset when I realized that through my work and my use of various corporate services I was actively, personally involved in the system doing the asset stripping.

Like a scream in the night, I sent off my thoughts to 100 close friends around the planet. They were folded up inside our annual Christmas letter - this was well before Facebook - along with a draft of the "Old Man in the Bag", a chapter of the book I had been trying to write in my spare time over the previous two decades to illustrate some of the power games we well-off folk were unintentionally forcing on others.

I was looking for some support for what I was thinking, and I was heartened by the sympathetic responses that some of my words generated. There was general agreement, for instance, even back then that the market place and our governments were leading us toward a dubious future. Everyone had their own theories about how and why, but their overall prognosis was the same. When I think back on it, I guess I should not have been surprised. They were, after all, close friends.

What I wrote started this way:

It is Monday, April 9th, 1990, a totally uninspiring autumn day in Taranaki. Although the greenhouse effect has generally brought improved weather to this side of the island, today it is grey and raining outside.

As I sit here typing this, I wonder what I will be doing next year at this time; what I will be doing in ten years time; what my children's children will be doing in a hundred years . . . Boy, is this classic mid-life crisis stuff, or what?

I am in a temporary lull at the moment with little to do except the never-ending cold call looking for new work and the occasional letter to write to someone over in Hastings or up in Auckland.

Though certainly one of the most enjoyable things I've ever done, my three year's work on the redesign of Hastings' central area is nearing its end, and I am nervous about what I will be able to find to replace it.

Maybe BECA Consultants will win the urban redesign project for Upper Hutt or Porirua and I'll have some steady work again. Or maybe Hawera will want me to give them a slide show on urban design possibilities next week, as they hinted yesterday. That at least would be a start.

I hate this part, not so much the waiting and wondering, though it's no fun, but the salesmanship part. The dark blue suits and ties that I cannot make myself wear, the elaborate ritualized duplicity, the cutthroat smiles of competitors. Mostly though, I hate the fact that there must always be winners and losers in this market game we all must play to survive. Actually, winning is not so bad, it's just the loosing that hurts!

I suppose I hate it mostly because in any competitive game, winners only win where there are losers, and I don't like the idea of getting ahead at some one else's expense, or losing when there is virtually no difference between us. What really is the significance of a thousandth of a second in a race except the color of the medal and the egos of the winners and losers?

I suppose it could also be because I know that the odds of winning in the market place are always stacked in favor of the most domineering, aggressive player, and I'm uncomfortable with the thought of having to live in a society where such attitudes are accepted as a fundamental requirement for survival.

I am uncomfortable with the thought that I must stand over the crowd unless I want it to stand over me. I wonder where this incredibly powerful force for societal stratification will ultimately take us all . . . to another India before the British . . . Or worse? Not that I don't enjoy standing out a little from the rest, but from a social perspective there is a difference between elevation and distance . . . isn't there?

Anyway, here I am thinking about the meaning of life and wondering if I'm crazy worrying about how many souls I am living off, and conversely, who is living off me. Funny, really, I am, after all, living in a fur lined rut yet again, aren't I? Who am I to complain? But is this really how I should be spending my life? . . . A parent message, if I ever heard one! What DID happen in my childhood? . . . Or should I be trying to figure out how to save the world?

The world doesn't really seem to be any worse today than it was yesterday. Anyone with such a ridiculous ambition as to suggest wanting to "SAVE" it, and with the even more ridiculous audacity to state it in writing, must be, by definition, totally mad, right? Or at least have a slightly??? over developed ego . . . or are they both the same thing?

I also cannot help thinking that even if the world really is stuffed up, why worry? It still may never go under. The reactive "Survival of the fittest" approach to life has managed to get humans this far. Somehow in its bloody history, the world has managed to deftly swing from one crisis to another, each time perhaps destroying a few valuable parts, but always recovering most of the original bits and eventually managing to find another usually improved direction to try, assuming that having an increased ability to manipulate ones environment is an improved direction.

Even the global pollution that continues to build and kill, and the nuclear holocaust that seems inevitable (if the past is any indication of the future) could simply be new forces acting on the pendulum that will help clean the slate at the peak of the swing, and allow the survivors in what ever life form they may find themselves, to swing back in an even better direction.

And it is hard to argue that this is not the best way to "progress" through indefinable time, for what is the pain and suffering of a few billion people over a few millennia given the scale of the universe? Is quality really any better than quantity?

Why interfere with the pendulum's swing, anyway? Whose purpose would it serve? Only my own ambition? Though people through planning can now grasp the seeds that control their future, who knows where the pendulum of chaos would swing if left alone. A game plan we controlled could well be worse than one we didn't. Although it may be difficult to sacrifice a person's happiness for the novelty of an unknown future, what is happiness? Can it be defined, or for that matter is happiness even the ultimate purpose of life? If not, what are we doing here? Does it matter if there is no purpose?

Is the only alternative to the unrestricted swings of the pendulum, the sterility of sameness and mediocrity; the loss of creativity, hope and ambition. Does stopping the excesses of the pendulum mean stopping the diversity and stimulation of life itself? Would it eliminate need, and without need, would there be no love?

I am putting all this drivel down in writing because I am fairly certain that before I die, I will be going somewhere with all the thoughts in my head about intercultural structures. I may eventually end up back near where I now sit, but I thought unless I put something down in writing at this point, undefined as it might be, farther down the path I won't really know if I am getting anywhere if there is nothing to compare the moment with.

For the record, I have been thinking about the meaning of life and the question to the answer 42 [from the Hitchhikers Guide to the Galaxy] for many years, though particularly the last five . . . since Helen decided to go back to school to finish becoming a Nurse, and manipulative me saw this as my ticket to finding global solutions.

My basic concern with the existing political / social / economic systems found around the world is that they don't think small enough to recognize, much less understand, the differences that exist between individual people and between cultures both within and between families, neighborhoods, communities and countries.

In my opinion, the various institutions of government, religion, justice, defense, commerce, education, health and environmental management around the world once set up to help relatively small groups of people deal with the problems of change in their own isolated, usually ecologically balanced, little spaces are now being called upon to juggle the very sophisticated requirements of a complex, very diverse global society, which not only has huge expectations but also very limited resources.

Through either arrogance, ignorance or the normal inherent inflexibility of most institutions, these now antiquated systems are having considerable, growing difficulty just surviving.

Democracies have certainly been an improvement over past systems, particularly with the freedoms of speech and religion they offer, but they are far from perfect, as the slums, street beggars, health problems, drug trade, crime, and other "immoralities" even within the wealthiest, most democratic countries of the world, amply demonstrate. And although there are still many good parts in these existing systems, particularly the more democratic ones, I believe things can only get worse, not better as time and technology march on, because there is at least one fundamental flaw in them all.

At the moment, almost no institutions except a few in isolated areas, use consensus as the means of reaching decisions on matters involving change. Given there are almost six billion people in the world, this is not surprising! Nevertheless, consensus is the only form of decision-making which can ensure that everyone accepts the decisions that are reached. It is also the only system that is capable of treating all minority interests with true equality.

Any other method of decision-making, even democratic decision-making, requires creating both "winners" and "losers" which unavoidably results in the subjugation of the less numerous, though not necessarily less right, minority group. In my opinion, as long as consensus is not used in public decision-making there can be no equality, and where there is no equality there can never be peace.

26

Consensus, of course, is difficult if not impossible to achieve among large groups, and it does not work very well in some commercial situations, which, in the past at least, made the existing alternative "democratic" systems a reasonable compromise.

But in today's technologically sophisticated world, decision-making which doesn't recognize the needs of up to nearly half those involved, means that there is considerable room for contempt, at the very least, among those whose needs are ignored.

To be able to use consensus decision-making, I believe any new intercultural structure must break up present day decision-making responsibilities into many more levels than exist at the moment. Nearly all of these need to be at a more local level than found in today's political / educational / judicial / religious / economic structures.

Probably not more than ten to fifteen people can be involved in any single decision. At the same time, however, I believe all decision-making systems must be integrated, as a decision in one area inevitably affects something else in another.

Thus, as I presently envision it, any new intercultural structure will probably require a fairly substantial change in the way we think about our institutions and how they work for us. For instance, I think it will require a change in how public space is controlled. For example. "public space" will probably need to be defined by use rather than ownership.

It may also require a change in how public and private activities are regulated, for example, how the media and special interest groups manipulate political decision-making, how physical and natural resources are managed and how movement and communication across space is directed. It may also involve how controversial personal behavior, such as birth control, suicide, euthanasia and drug abuse is dealt with, and where discrimination / prejudice can / cannot be tolerated.

The new structure(s) will have to be able to operate among any group of people with any level of education or access to technology, although the more sophisticated the education and/or technology, the easier for participants to freely exchange information and thus reach decisions.

Checks and balances to protect individuals and the public in general from excesses of the system(s), or from any other abuse of power such as from any conflict resolution which condones injustice or social inequity, will have to be built into the system too. However, I do not believe it will require the cumbersome and in my opinion, antiquated, lawyer dominated system now found in the West.

At this point, of course, I am not at all sure of any of these details. I only believe that the ultimate survival of humanity, if indeed this can ever be a mutually agreed goal, will require that eventually we must all live together by mutual consent, not by the exercise of power.

No peoples social structure, culture or mores . . . no economical, philosophical, religious, legal or political system can include as a fundamental premise, the pitting of one man against another. It cannot require one person to lose before another may gain, despite the fact that this is consistent with the "survival of the fittest" philosophy.

I don't doubt that formulating a system that stimulates creativity and accepts ideological diversity in a market setting without this as a fundamental premise will inevitably require some sacrifice of individual rights, but that's nothing new. The abolition of murder by law required the sacrifice of an individual's right to resolve certain personal conflicts by direct action.

However, I think there is something fundamental in the difference between personal rights taken by others, and personal rights freely given up by the individuals involved.

A solution is there, I am sure of it; probably many of them. It is just a little more subtle and elusive than capitalism or communism or socialism or fascism or any other 'ism' or religion now preached although all of the above I think have valuable lessons to teach us in the way it all might work.

In addition, I do not believe that any solution should require the sacrifice of a revolution to achieve. Indeed if it does, my search will have failed in one of its most basic objectives: peace.

On the other hand, even in my most optimistic mood, any solution will require a radical change in thinking, which could take generations to achieve. And I suppose someday someone may well look back with the wisdom of time and see that whatever comes of this, if indeed anything does, was all only another predictable swing in the path of the perpetually swinging pendulum.

Chapter 3:

Making Public Decisions with Guns and Money: *discusses two of the primary ways existing governments now make decisions; through war or its threat, and through the market place. It includes a UN chart which obliquely points out that over the last 20 years the USA could have unilaterally ended virtually all of the major problems facing humanity on this planet, by providing clean water, clean energy, food, education, health care and housing to literally every one in need on the planet, along with stopping climate change, eliminating all land mines and nuclear weapons, and paying off all developing nation debt, had it used just part of its existing military budget to help the world rather than fight it "defending democracy".*

I know that consensus does not work in large groups. Any large Quaker meeting that tries to grapple with a contentious issue admirably demonstrates the difficulties, despite being well managed and friendly.

However, I'd like to step back from a discussion about the practicality of using consensus decision-making in our existing public institutions for a moment to talk first about some of the other decision-making techniques we now use around this planet. They each have their own good and bad points.

To start with, let's be clear. Public decision-making in any form today is about power. This was not always the case, and in rare instances, it still isn't as I will elaborate upon in chapter 6. However, in most governments and other public institutions today, decision-making is essentially about who gets to decide what happens to us next; about where our tax money goes; about who gets to spend it; about who wins and who loses.

There are currently at least a half dozen ways to make public decisions. The most expensive and disruptive technique we now use, one that is also least recognized as a public decision-making technique, is war.

War is used to decide big questions in the same way murder was once used to decide small ones. Thankfully, most of humankind has accepted that murder rarely leads to a lasting solution, but too few yet accept that war has the same unreliability for problem solving.

For the last few decades, or the last ten millennia since civilization began some would say, war, or its threat, has been the public decision-making technique of choice. If in doubt, consider the amount of money most countries spend today resolving problems peacefully compared with the amount of money they spend on their military.

My wife and I were living in the United States when the 9/11 disaster happened in New York. Only three weeks earlier, we had taken a British nephew to the top of the World Trade Center to show him the sights. We were working in Philadelphia at the time while I was researching this book and trying to decide if we'd made a mistake leaving the US 25 years earlier.

When it happened, I could not believe it, watching the buildings fall and people leaping to their deaths on our television screen as if it were a Hollywood horror movie.

A few days later, on the way back from my mother's coincidental funeral in Salt Lake City just after the airports had re-opened, out of morbid curiosity my wife and I climbed out of the Wall Street subway station in Manhattan through the smell of acrid smoke into two inches of white powder covering everything. It was there among the horror that I began to wonder whether something positive could come out of the catastrophe.

Perhaps, I thought, the US Government could hold off seeking revenge for a moment to see why some people held such anger against America. Already Iraq and Saddam Hussein were being named as the perpetrators of the attack.

It was what I had been trying to write about for three decades in my book "The Old Man in the Bag" - that money and power, even when their use is well intentioned, can sometimes generate anger and hate among those on the receiving end.

The New York disaster could have been such a public learning experience; a healing experience. Instead the US Government and media just labeled the 9/11 criminals as "insane" to explain their behavior and left it at that.

While the terrorists and their sponsors had done something truly horrific and certainly deserved to be punished, it did not seem to me there was anything insane about their actions. They were simply seeking revenge for what the sometimes overly self-focused American Government, American corporations and American culture had done to them, their families, and their own culture for some time.

Depressed by the US Government's response, early in the new year my wife and I decided to return to the more socially inclusive reality of New Zealand, but not before visiting the United Nations to get a glimpse of one of this planet's few remaining hopes for peace.

On the wall of an upstairs hall in the main UN building, I found a chart that still haunts me to this day. It graphically pointed out that globally we spend considerably more on beating each other up than on fixing the reasons why we do. (See page 33)

The poster did not explain how it came up with the figures it contained, so when we finally made it back to New Zealand I tried to recalculate some of them myself. It was clear there had been quite a number of assumptions used in their creation, but I could not find anything drastically wrong with any of them.

What still haunts me is knowing that for much of the last two decades since then, America's spending on its military has been almost half the planet's total expenditure on weapons and war; enough to completely fix the planet on its own! Even today its spending on defense is more than the seven next highest defense spenders in the world combined; that is, more than China, Russia, the United Kingdom, Germany, France, Saudi Arabia and India, put together.

I cannot help thinking that if the US had spent just 60-70% of its own existing military budget helping the planet over the last 20 years rather than fighting it, America alone could have virtually ended all hunger, poverty and illiteracy on this planet. It could have provided not only food and education for all of humanity in need, but also housing and health care including AIDS control throughout the world . . . even to all its own poor.

I don't mean, if America had helped just its friends or if it had spent everything it had. I mean if it had spent only part of its military budget and left all its other internal and external programs untouched, it could have completely changed the entire planet for the better.

In addition to ending all poverty everywhere, that same piece of the US military budget, according to the UN figures, could have also stabilized global population growth, prevented global warming, stopped global deforestation, paid off all developing nation debt, removed all land mines, eliminated nuclear weapons and perhaps most importantly, provided clean safe energy for all; that is, ended the world's dependence on fossil fuels.

For substantially less than what the US Government alone has spent on its military over the last two decades, it could have ended any need for its armies to be in the Middle East, Europe, Asia or, for that matter, anywhere else in the world. It could have eliminated both the motivation behind global terrorism and the need for its nearly 800 existing overseas military installations now protecting its interests outside the US. It also could have saved its own taxpayers hundreds of billions of dollars a year and possibly avoided making any further enemies at the same time

However, most politicians in both major American political parties chose a much more expensive path. Using the 9-11 terror attack on New York as justification, they have reinforced and exaggerated a culture of fear across the country and the world to justify continuing their overly excessive, globally provocative expenditure on America's military.

This is exactly what a well-loved American president had predicted sixty years ago. In his farewell speech to the American public at the end of his presidency in 1960, the former WWII military commander and two-term US President, Dwight D Eisenhower spoke about his serious concern over maintaining a standing army in the USA after WWII ended.

In February, 2002, on a corridor wall in the United Nations in New York. I photographed the poster below accurately recreated here:

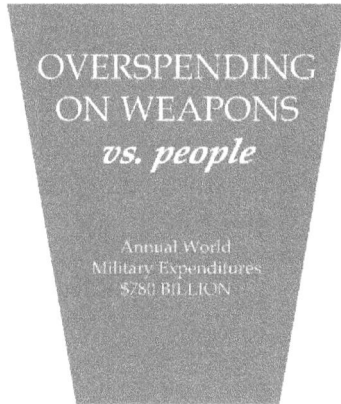

OVERSPENDING
ON WEAPONS
vs. people

Annual World
Military Expenditures
$780 BILLION

Original photo

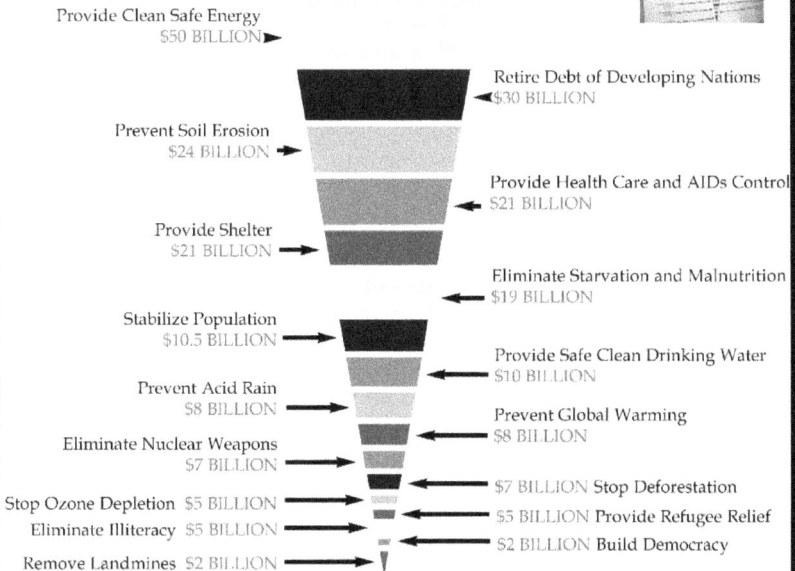

Provide Clean Safe Energy
$50 BILLION ▶

Retire Debt of Developing Nations
◀ $30 BILLION

Prevent Soil Erosion
$24 BILLION ▶

Provide Health Care and AIDs Control
◀ $21 BILLION

Provide Shelter
$21 BILLION ▶

Eliminate Starvation and Malnutrition
◀ $19 BILLION

Stabilize Population
$10.5 BILLION ▶

Provide Safe Clean Drinking Water
◀ $10 BILLION

Prevent Acid Rain
$8 BILLION ▶

Prevent Global Warming
$8 BILLION

Eliminate Nuclear Weapons
$7 BILLION ▶

◀ $7 BILLION Stop Deforestation

Stop Ozone Depletion $5 BILLION ▶

◀ $5 BILLION Provide Refugee Relief

Eliminate Illiteracy $5 BILLION ▶

◀ $2 BILLION Build Democracy

Remove Landmines $2 BILLION ▶

Above are annual costs of various global programs for solving the major needs and environmental problems facing humanity. Each program is the amount needed to accomplish the goal for all in need in the world. Their combined total cost is approximately 30% of the worlds total annual military expenditure.

© United Nations 2002

His speech has become known by those outside the USA as the "Eisenhower Prophesy". Up until that war, America had only a very small permanent armed force. However, President Eisenhower was concerned that America's rapidly enlarging Military/ Industrial/Congressional Complex, as he called it, might become so commercially and politically indispensable to the Country's economy that it would bias the American Government's problem solving toward military solutions rather than peaceful ones.

He feared congressional representatives would see they could buy votes and secure their own political futures by bringing in large military contracts to those who voted for them or to the corporations who helped finance their election campaigns.

This certainly seems to be what has happened. The horse-trading between representatives over defense contracts within the Appropriations Committees of both Houses is now globally well-known and the subject of Hollywood movies.

Those in government know that wars need not be expensive for everyone. They can be very lucrative for the corporations making and selling weapons and for the soldiers not maimed or killed in them. It is only everyone else who has to pay for war.

§

Speaking of expensive decision-making, a second significant way of making public decisions that can have almost the same impact on some as war, is capitalism, colloquially known as the "market place".

The now globally pervasive system of economics probably outranks war as the most powerful decision-making tool on the planet today, although its effects are usually a bit more subtle. For most governments, both national and local, it has become the primary way to decide important matters. For public corporations it is now virtually the only method used to make decisions.

The power of the market place is most obvious, strangely enough, in countries that consider themselves "Christian". The Prophet, Jesus, threw the moneylenders out of the temple and got himself martyred because of his disgust over its corrupting influence on society. He felt the Jewish method of charging interest on borrowed money was inherently immoral and the best way to deal with its power was by following God's teachings.

Islam was founded for virtually the same reason. The only significant difference between the two was that the prophet Mohammed came up with a detailed way to resist the power of the market place and protect the morals of humanity from the moneylenders by setting up laws and a government decision-making structure that had both morality and control of the market place built into it. Among other things it banned charging time based interest on borrowed money, and still does.

Christianity tried hard to resist accepting the Jewish view of money lending (of charging interest on loans) for more than a thousand years. The original motivation behind the establishment of pawn shops and other similar lending facilities was to get around Christianity's objection to money lending that included interest charges.

Among Catholics, usury was an excommunicable offence until quite recently.

The birth of the Protestant religion in the 16th century was at least partly driven by the desire of some Christians to be able to lend money and charge interest the same way that Jews did. In the end even the leaders of the Catholic Church finally gave in to the "immorality" of interest based money lending despite the views of their Messiah.

The market place isn't all bad, of course. It can play a very important role in finding efficient solutions to problems involving time. Unlike any religion, philosophy or more formal government structure, it is a universal global public decision-making system. It is probably the most efficient, self sufficient, self-perpetuating human institution on the planet today.

It is also very compatible with democratic decision-making. It tends to turn public choice into black and white values in the same way majority vote decision-making does.

Most of the time the characteristics of the market place can be positive, but at times its emphasis on economic efficiency can have a social cost, such as in the operation of hospitals, schools and other institutions reliant on cooperation among their staff.

For instance, hospitals that use competitive economic

reward (the market place) to motivate their staff subtly discourage them from sharing their knowledge with each other. Individual knowledge is worth money. Sharing it could cost them their jobs when the economy gets tough. Patient health care is the inevitable loser.

Teachers who have to compete economically with other teachers for their jobs may instill in their students the value of competition by their behavior, but not the value of cooperation. The former is a necessity to be successful in the market place; the latter can be an impediment in it, although it is fundamental to achieving peace and making livable communities in the world.

The market place also has serious difficulty looking at long-term solutions to environmental or social problems. In fact, time always has a cost penalty in the market place in the form of interest. Interest charges virtually force people, businesses, communities, even whole countries that use economics as the primary basis of their decision-making, to choose short-term solutions over long-term solutions.

Sustainability and society are virtually the antitheses of what the market place engenders.

America's development history this century demonstrates many examples of short-term economics based decision-making and the limitations of the market place in protecting the physical and social environment.

One of the more obvious, from my own town planning perspective, is the demise of America's town centers. Despite the advice of many well-educated and well-motivated land use planners, since the 1960s virtually all American town centers have declined significantly. Some of them have literally disappeared altogether.

The Wal-Marts and Costcos of America have been blamed for their death, but they are only a symptom of the problem, not the cause.

Seventy years ago, the rapid rise in automobile ownership and the resulting traffic congestion in American town centers were crippling them. Most professionals doing public planning in the US advised local politicians that the establishment of suburban commercial strip malls would be a very poor solution to downtown traffic congestion problems. What was needed was better management of transportation networks, particularly mass transportation systems, public roads and public parking, within and around town centers.

Town centers, they said, already had significant public investment in them in the form of existing public buildings, roads, railways, public utilities and a myriad of public institutions, as well as considerable public history and sense of place in them.

They warned the politicians that the cost of commercial strip developments would not only be just the relocation of traffic congestion into the suburbs, but the demise of nodal based transport services like railroads, and with it the end of efficiently provided housing, business, public utilities and public services.

This was also what most professionals responsible for land use planning in other developed countries told their politicians when they faced the same dilemma with growing local use of private cars. Today, anyone who does much overseas travelling can easily see who listened and who did not.

For the most part, all suburban strip mall developments have done for America is make a few developers very rich, primarily because they did not have to pay for the new roads, utilities and public services networks that eventually had to be built nearby to support them.

Suburban land was cheap, and it was easy for American politicians to listen to the corporate logic that strip malls would immediately reduce the price of goods for local residents.

The market place offered politicians a simple way to make their decisions. The short-term benefit was easy to calculate and the long-term cost to the overall community was difficult to quantify. Most long-term costs, like the physical and social loss of a community's heart, were simply ignored.

§

Cynics would also suggest that towns without hearts fit in well with America's strong legal support for the rights of individuals over the rights of communities under the US Constitution.

Back in the late 1700s when the US Constitution was being written, the most important concern of the day was protecting the rights of individuals. As a result, the collective rights of communities got no mention in either it or in America's Bill of Rights.

Corporate lawyers of today know this. Any well-intentioned American planner invariably finds him or herself up against a brick wall when trying to protect the public interest if a local developer does not think there is a buck in it for himself.

What sealed the fate of American town centers was that unlike almost every other developed country in the world, the US has no national planning legislation. There is no serious effort anywhere to balance corporate power in the market place with the collective interests of communities.

Most individual states have some planning legislation but even the best of them, like Oregon and Florida have had to limit the support they can give to communities and the public interest because of the inherent bias of the Constitution in favor of individual rights.

US corporations have had it all handed to them, literally, as they are considered "individuals" under US law, even if they have no morals, no social conscience and literally no real interest in their communities other than financial.

Not only does this mean corporations can use constitutional law to help prove they have the right to put strip malls anywhere they choose, unlike communities, but they also usually have more money than most communities to search the planet for credible experts to overwhelm any argument a community might put up in court to try to stop them.

The market place versus community interest has been a very sad, one-sided battle in US courts for the last half century, and the death of America's town centers is one of the more obvious, direct consequences.

Chapter 4:

Other Ways We Make Public Decisions: *discusses Aristotle's six forms of government including Democracies, which the Greek philosopher describes as a "corruption". It also describes New Zealand's unique form of government which has no permanent over-riding constitution, no publicly elected head of state and only one legislative chamber, forty percent of whose members are not publicly elected.*

War and the market place aside, the Greek philosopher, Aristotle, recognized six methods of public decision-making or types of government. These were monarchies, aristocracies, polities, tyrannies, oligarchies and democracies. He dismissed the second three as corruptions of the first three.

Although once the dominant form of government in the world, there are few monarchies left today. Those that still exist usually have titles that include "Kingdom" or "Sultanate" unless they are the result of an unexpected army coup. They are seen by most people outside them to run on the whim of just one person, so it would be easy to think they could not have much trouble making public decisions.

The reality, however, is that modern day monarchies are rarely run by just one person. Those running them have just as much trouble making public decisions as those running any other form of government. The difficulty is that for the public, the political "whims" of those actually running monarchies are hard to predict, much less rely on.

In the mid 1990s I worked in Brunei for a year designing a new town and preparing a land use plan for one of its districts. Ostensibly, I was working for one of the richest men in the world, the Sultan of Brunei. The reports and articles I had read before I got there said that he lived in the largest house in the world and that he owned more land in Australia than found in his own country.

I smile now when I think of it. The truth was nothing like the technically accurate words that described the situation. The really nice, very small (in stature) leader of Brunei struck me as being more akin to Plato's benevolent dictator than the hype of wealth and power that painted him otherwise.

Most of the Sultan's money was in name only. The entire country of Brunei survived on the oil found off shore. All of the oil contracts were in the Sultan's name because he was the official Head of State, but he used most of "his" money to pay for the British style bureaucracy that actually ran the Country.

In Brunei when I was there, almost half of all those employed in the Country were paid either directly or indirectly by the Sultan. Oil money paved the roads. Oil money built and ran the free public hospitals and schools. Oil money built all the gorgeous places of worship. It even paid for a huge Disneyland style amusement park that the local people could enjoy for free.

While he lived with one of his wives in part of a 1,788-room mansion, it was also where his senior ministers met and conducted state affairs, and where foreign visitors were housed and entertained. The farm in the vast Australian Outback just raised beef to feed Bruneians. It was hard to raise healthy cattle in Brunei's own sweltering heat.

The Sultan's views generally did make it into government decision-making, but rarely directly, and probably not always in ways he intended. One of my first jobs was to undertake a survey of the people already living in the area where the new town was proposed. Although it was the first local planning survey ever undertaken in the Country, the Government agreed to all the questions I suggested, including asking local residents what they liked and disliked about where they lived, and how they thought things could be improved.

A considerable amount of time and money was spent interviewing every single one of the 500 existing households in the area, and in the end, the survey found out about a number of interesting local problems, opportunities and desires. The first draft of the district's first-ever local plan tried hard to deal with them.

What was hoped, and what officials had originally agreed, was that the results of the poll and the draft plan they had inspired would then be taken back to the local people to find out what they thought about the ideas. I have always been an advocate of the "Delphi Technique", a conflict resolution tool that involves exchanging ideas among all concerned more than once to work out the most mutually acceptable outcome.

The plan was first reviewed and approved as a draft by all appropriate officials, but literally the day before the public meeting was to be held, it was called off. I doubt the Sultan himself was worried about it, but it was clear other lesser officials did not really like the idea of involving the public in such a direct way.

The Sultan's biggest worry at the time was being overthrown by his brother. I had considerable difficulty getting hold of any digitized maps to create plans for the new town because he was afraid they'd be used to organize a coup d'état against him.

In the end, his worry was justified although the maps I eventually obtained were not the cause of his demise. His brother, whom the Sultan had appointed Finance Minister to try to keep him happy, emptied the royal treasury on whimsical investments not long after this. With the bad investments went any chance of implementing most of the plan the locals had suggested, or for that matter, most of the Sultan's plans for the Country as a whole for a while either.

§

The larger Sultanates might be better described under Aristotle's classification of government types as Aristocracies rather than monarchies, as they generally have more than one ruler. None of them is democratic but the decisions they make are not technically the consequence of just one leader either. Like one-ruler governments, they all take thousands of mid level bureaucrats, making thousands of public decisions daily to run.

China and many other countries pose similar difficulties in classifying their decision-making type. Most have some aristocratic elements in them, but to a greater or lesser degree most also contain some democratic elements as well.

Aristotle's definition of the third form of government; a polity, is a government focused on meeting the common interests of the public rather than focused on private corporate interests. Even those governments that consider themselves entirely democratic like the USA and Great Britain contain elements which are not focused on the public interest but on the interests of those controlling government, such as corporations. And those that insist they are, are rarely based on the "one person, one vote" principle.

In the American Senate for instance, it takes the votes of nearly 70 Californian residents to equal the vote of just one Wyoming resident, and in Britain's House of Lords, decision-making is almost entirely by the wealthy and elite since its membership is largely through inheritance or appointment.

Of all the governments that consider themselves democratic, New Zealand may be among the better ones. It is often singled out by global public watchdogs as one of the least corrupt in the world; corruption being one of the better indicators of government manipulation by private, non-democratic special interest groups.

Some might find this endorsement of New Zealand's government extremely difficult to believe, given the way it actually works. It lacks many of the usual "checks and balances" that other democratic countries consider essential to govern.

Every single national politician in the New Zealand Government is elected every three years, so its ongoing continuity could easily be a problem. It does not have two "houses" or political decision making bodies like many democracies have so there is no separate, independent review of new legislation, and the Country's leader is not directly elected by the people, unlike most presidents. Most significantly, there is no sacrosanct written constitution, so there is no ultimate law to guide government decisions.

There is an independent judicial system that interprets existing law, but judges cannot create new laws by reinterpreting them as the US Supreme Court does with the American Constitution from time to time. If a New Zealand judge decides to interpret a law differently from the way current politicians interpret it, the politicians simply reword the law so there is no room for doubt.

New Zealand uses a system of proportional representation which has aspects of the "Sortition" version of democracy proposed by Dr Brett Hennig in 2015, where all representatives are randomly selected from the general populace, avoiding many of the pitfalls of current election methods.

Literally 40% of all New Zealand's central government politicians are not elected. They are selected by the members of a political party on the basis of their personal knowledge and experience, and the number of them pulled into government depends on the overall number of votes which that party receives.

All politicians in a political party are pledged to vote the same way on any law change except on rare conscience votes. Consequently, any majority party or coalition of parties elected to run the Government has the power to change every single law and piece of legislation in the Country at any time.

However, that does not happen, partly because financial support and media exposure of those running for office are very tightly controlled and independent of political manipulation. It also doesn't happen because in New Zealand, the public's belief in individual freedom is still balanced by a strong public belief in social justice and community interest. The New Zealand public's widespread support of the government's efforts to deal with the recent Covid-19 global pandemic demonstrated this well.

Such loosely managed government decision-making has allowed New Zealand to lead the world in the introduction of a number of social reforms. It was the first country in the world to give women the right to vote, the first to set eight hours as the length of a standard working day and one of the first to introduce universal social security for the elderly.

New Zealanders have had publicly funded universal health care and unemployment insurance for several generations. People who are sick, injured or unemployed for any reason can be assured of receiving enough government support to live on until they can work again, however long this may take, even if it is forever.

The most listened to radio and TV channels are state owned, but they are meticulously separated from political interference. It was once even better. Unfortunately, thirty years ago all state owned television channels were commercialized when the Country went through its financial meltdown. Now they have to compete for corporate advertising finance to survive.

Today, like everywhere else in the world, the not-so-subtle culture, beliefs and institutional pressures of the international market place now influence the contents of almost all media in New Zealand and thus the minds of everyone who reads, watches or listens to them.

§

The Country's widespread, ill-considered adoption of overseas business practices and its government's right winged policies over the last 3 decades have led New Zealand to a seriously widening gap between the rich and poor.

Its once effective social support systems have struggled to survive as taxes on the rich have steadily fallen under successive Governments professing to "save" the Country from its debt burden. Up until recently most New Zealanders believed in the American economic "trickle down" theory despite increasing proof that it only works in reverse, to benefit the rich.

Thankfully this may be starting to change. In New Zealand's 2017 general election there was a striking shift back to a more socially sympathetic central government. The new Government was a coalition of 3 parties; the main liberal "Labor" party, the small environmental "Green" party and another small usually right leaning "swing" party known as "New Zealand First".

Amazingly, it was the leader of that party, Winston Peters, who started the change. He was New Zealand's longest serving politician when he announced why his party chose to support the left leaning coalition this time, by saying:

> *"Far too many New Zealanders have come to view today's capitalism, not as their friend, but as their foe. And they are not all wrong."*

His sentiment was then reinforced by the young Labor Party leader, Jacinda Ardern, who almost overnight brought back a social conscience into Government decision making. The focus of the Coalition Government's first major budget wasn't on raising GDP (Gross Domestic Product) as is the focus of most county's politicians, but on improving New Zealander's "wellness", including mental and physical health, housing and education.

§

Unfortunately, while New Zealand has a very flexible, responsive and internationally acclaimed form of government, it is still vulnerable to the same decision-making mistakes other majority vote based democracies make.

Every democratic government in the world is different, of course, but to explain the vulnerability of New Zealand's government to poor decision-making, I first need to explain a bit about the Country and its history.

New Zealand contains about 5 million people (in 2021) and 100,000 square miles of land. It contains about the same area of land as the State of Colorado in the USA, although it contains slightly fewer people. It is blessed with similar mountain ranges and plains as those found in that state, but it contains a number of other geographic features that aren't in Colorado, like fjords, volcanoes and rain forests.

It is also surrounded by water rather than land and is a long way from anywhere. If the point of a compass were centered on New Zealand and an arc drawn with a 6,000 mile (10,000 kilometer) radius or twice the distance from New York to London, the arc would just reach the edge of South East Asia but would still be well short of most other large land areas including North America, South America, Africa and India.

The only land areas of any size within the arc would be Australia, 1200 miles (2,000 kilometers) to the west, and Antarctica, a similar distance to the south.

The most obvious consequence of New Zealand's isolation and diverse landform is its very unusual collection of plants and animals, many of which are unique in the world.

Partly because of this, and partly because of its late colonization, New Zealand has been a world leader in comprehensive sustainable land use planning.

Its very first colonial settlements back in the 1840s were planned communities, often complete with greenbelts 50 years before the Garden City movement began in Europe. Its first comprehensive national planning legislation was passed in 1926, and in the early 1950s land use planning was made mandatory across every city, town and rural area in the country.

In the 1970s more advanced national planning laws were enacted to protect a much wider range of health, safety, economic, social and environmental aspects of the public interest.

Then in 1991, more than 90 existing New Zealand Acts and Regulations where brought together under a single new Resource Management Act based on the concept of the

"Sustainable Management of Natural and Physical Resources".

It was a "left-wing" Government that drafted the new national planning legislation. However, when a "right-wing" Government was brought back into power in the next public election, it could have been thrown out before ever being put into law, but it wasn't. By that time, most New Zealanders on all sides of the political spectrum recognized that the sustainable use of resources was a concept that was fundamentally important to everyone's future

One of the things that lead to the introduction of the concept of environmental sustainability in the Country's planning legislation was the New Zealand Government's ultimately disastrous "Think Big" development decisions made in the early 1980s when the Country was trying to find a way out of its very severe economic crisis.

What could have been a godsend but nearly resulted in the Country's bankruptcy, was the discovery of a large natural gas field off the west coast of the North Island. The Government had signed a "take or pay" agreement with the gas field's discoverer in order to persuade the company to undertake the risky exploration. With the gas discovery, however, the agreement forced the Government to quickly decide how to use it.

At the time, gasoline (petrol) was an expensive import for New Zealand and car ownership, second only to the US per capita, was rapidly rising despite the economy. The price of petrol was already more than twice the price Americans paid for it. Compounding the immediate problem, there was a sudden global shortage of crude oil and New Zealanders were forced to ration all the petrol they could import.

With Government assistance, New Zealanders quickly converted about 10% of their vehicles to run on the new locally available natural gas fuel. However, around the time of the oil shortage, Mobile Oil discovered a catalyst that could convert methanol, made from methane, the primary component of New Zealand's natural gas, into synthetic gasoline.

Through skilful lobbying, it convinced the New Zealand Government that it would be better to convert the newly discovered gas to gasoline than to encourage more vehicles to convert to natural gas. As a liquid, they argued, it would be easier for everyone to use and it would guarantee that the Country could meet its "take or pay" commitment.

There was substantial opposition to the idea from environmentalists, particularly when it was discovered that literally half of the energy in the gas would be lost in its conversion to synthetic gasoline, but despite serious opposition in Parliament, the Government had majority support (as always) so it decided to undertake the 2.5 billion dollar project anyway. At that point, it was the single most expensive public project the New Zealand Government had ever undertaken.

The Government was seriously pressed for time so it decided to modify the existing planning legislation so it could get through the necessary court hearings faster. It did not scrimp on doing its homework for the project, though. It still spent a considerable amount of money and effort choosing the right site for the plant, using technical experts from around the world.

Eventually, after investigating more than 30 possible sites, project planners settled on a large, flat, isolated coastal site for the plant for three main reasons:

1. The giant structural components of the plant, fabricated overseas, could be off loaded directly onto shore without impacting the nearby city and its port.

2. The coastal location would also allow the relatively clean, treated effluent from the plant to be directly discharged into the turbulent Tasman Sea for immediate dilution and dispersion.

3. The site's sandy ground would provide good support for the massive structures the plant would contain.

In addition to the environmentalists, local Maori protested against the proposed plant because its sewage outfall would go through one of their most important shellfish beds.

The Government could demonstrate, scientifically, that the treated water discharged through the outfall would be harmless to the environment. The Maori, however, said it did not matter how harmless the chemicals were, the water would still be spiritually tainted. As a result, they could not eat any shellfish near the outfall, and the loss of their significant food resource would in turn seriously jeopardize the "mana" or reputation of local Maori and undermine their cultural identity.

There were appeals lodged by both local Maori and the environmentalists under the fast-track planning legislation, but the planning and legal judges dismissed virtually all of them.

High-level political intervention in the form of New Zealand's Prime Minister, eventually persuaded the plant to redirect its effluent temporarily through another existing outfall onto an already contaminated shellfish bed until a land based treatment system could be provided, but despite the best advice available, the huge project still proved to be a complete financial disaster.

The new fuel turned out to be so pure it could not be used in most vehicles and it was cheaper to continue importing fuel and selling the new synthetic gasoline to someone overseas who could use it directly than modify it further to work in local vehicles.

The Government never even recovered its initial investment, much less made a profit from the plant. It was eventually forced to pay a private corporation more than a hundred million dollars just to take it off its hands.

What was worse from an environmental planning point of view, all three of the primary reasons for choosing the original plant site eventually proved either incorrect or irrelevant.

Not only did the site on the coast prove unnecessary because of the use of an alternative outfall (Much to the consternation of local Maori, it took nearly 40 years for the alternative outfall to be replaced by the promised land based treatment system), it proved unnecessary for getting overseas plant modules onto the shore.

Shortly before plant fabrication started, the project economists calculated that it would be cheaper to fix up the load bearing capacity of the local road system and truck the four stories high, block long modules overland on huge transporters from the nearby city's existing port.

The third main reason for choosing the site, the stability of the land, simply proved inaccurate. The sand turned out to be waterlogged and so unstable that the entire site had to be ringed with high volume permanently running pumps so that the site would not liquefy in an earthquake. There was an active volcano just 30 miles (50 km) away.

The national fiasco pointed out on a grand scale something I have observed repeatedly throughout my planning career; that even with the best minds, the most compelling scientific evidence, and the most meticulously followed legal protocols, solving just the problems of the majority without meeting the needs of everyone affected, rarely ever permanently solves anything.

Chapter 5:

The Delphi Technique: *is about how I helped a very diverse range of technical experts, government officials, industry representatives and more than two dozen social, cultural and environmental organizations work together to identify the site for a very contentious major petrochemical complex in New Zealand following the discovery of natural gas off-shore there.*

The serious risk inherent in majority vote decision-making was not the only thing I learned back in the 1980s during the time of New Zealand's "Think Big" projects. Around the time the site selection process for the original "Gas to Gasoline" plant was nearing completion, I was asked by the Government to help them identify a site for a second stage of petrochemical developments in the same part of the Country using the same resource.

The Government had concluded that other industrial developments using the newly discovered natural gas were likely in the future. These developments included a gas liquids extraction plant, a synthetic aviation fuels plant and a polypropylene or polyethylene manufacturing plant producing 300,000 tons of plastic a year and employing up to 900 people.

It was estimated that the anticipated industries would require up to 750 acres (300 hectares) of land, including the buffer zone around them.

The earlier site selection study had taken a lot of time and money and even at that point, it was clear there would remain considerable opposition to it. So I asked the not yet closed Planning Division of the Government's Ministry of Works if they'd be willing to try another planning approach.

In August, 1983, I wrote a brief report to the Taranaki Regional Council and the Government's Ministry of Works which described the Delphi Technique and how it might be possible to get a better, faster, less expensive decision with more local support if they were willing to try it. Much to their credit, they both readily agreed to its use.

As soon as possible, the heads of all organizations and Government Departments that had shown an interest in the first site selection study were approached and asked if they would like to be involved in a second one, right from the start.

They were warned that their involvement would require putting their views in writing and publicly sharing (for free) all information they used to form their views, whether technical or subjective.

Though some, like the local Maori and the environmentalists, were still angry by what had recently happened in the first site selection process, they all liked the idea of being involved right from the beginning, so virtually everyone said yes.

In fact, the original twelve groups first approached grew rapidly until in the end there were 42 groups involved, including Government departments, quasi-public agencies, and local special interest groups.

They included five land resource management organizations, five water resource management organizations, seven transport and infrastructure organizations, seven cultural and social organizations, eight environmental protection organizations, four local governments, four major industrial and commercial interests, and two valuation and design providers.

The process was started by providing everyone involved with everything known about the proposed developments and giving them detailed maps with notes on them showing where several possible sites might be.

Each group then wrote back and explained where they thought their preferred site would be, if any, and why. Some said there was no site that would be suitable and why, but then when pressed were willing to identify a site which they thought would be least objectionable. Almost all provided considerable technical information to back up their views.

Everything each group provided, including preferred site and all background information, was duplicated and then sent back to everyone involved along with a matrix setting out everyone's basic information and an initial conclusion of what it all meant.

Each group then reconsidered its views after considering all the new information and then revised or added to their original submissions. All new material was distributed among all involved as before and any changes to initial responses were requested. This process was repeated until no one felt they had anything new to add.

In the end, a particular site did stand out and it eventually was put forward as the study's recommended site for the Stage II developments. Local environmentalists never did like the whole idea of the project but they ended up at least comfortable that the site ultimately chosen was as good as they could have hoped.

Virtually everyone involved praised the process, including the Government, who had found a solution to its industrial site location question in a quarter of the time and

STAGE II SITE STUDY

A PUBLIC ANALYSIS OF ALTERNATIVE SITES FOR POSSIBLE FUTURE PETROCHEMICAL DEVELOPMENTS IN THE GREATER WAITARA AREA

at a fraction of the cost of the first study.

I had used the Delphi Technique before, but it was the first time I had used it to deal with a relatively significant, contentious problem. It showed me that some of the principals of consensus decision-making are realistic, even if it requires keeping down the numbers of those involved.

Chapter 6:

Lessons From The South Pacific:

is about the centuries old Samoan practice of making community decisions by consensus. It is where I learned first hand during several years living and working among the local people there trying to plan for climate change induced sea level rise, that it does not require unanimous or even majority support to make consensus decisions.

It was not until 2005 that I began to understand the full power of consensus decision-making. In that year I started a two year contract in Samoa helping nearly 150 local communities create coastal management plans to improve their resilience to natural disasters like cyclones, flooding, land slip and global warming induced sea level rise.

In the early 1990s two major cyclones had ravaged the Country and destroyed a number of coastal towns and villages. Although few people had died in the catastrophes, the natural disasters generated considerable interest in improving how the Country might handle others in the future.

At the time, I didn't know much about Samoa or its culture. I only knew Samoa, formerly known as Western Samoa, was administered by New Zealand until it gained its independence in the early 1960s. I didn't know that missionaries had converted everyone there to Christianity by the mid 1800s and it was now a very dominant part of their culture; that in 1900 Germany had negotiated with the US and Britain the right to colonize Samoa in exchange for the US getting American Samoa and Britain getting Tonga; and that during the early days of WWI, New Zealand had bloodlessly removed the Germans on instruction from England.

Actually, it was not that bloodless, although no Germans were shot in the takeover. In 1918, New Zealand inadvertently let in someone with the Spanish Flu, which ended up killing over 20% of the entire Samoan population. This left a lasting memory among Samoans of the bad things foreigners could introduce to their land, even if done accidentally.

One of the unique things about Samoa today is that almost no land in the entire country is privately owned. There is some land in saleable titles scattered in and around the capitol city, Apia, and some of the missions are built on land they've managed to get title to over the last century and a half, but that's it. Less than 2% of Samoa can be bought and sold; and then only to other local Samoans.

Some parts of Samoa are owned by the Samoan Government. There's a national park, a hydro dam and scattered remnants of old plantations once owned by the Germans now under Government control, but most of Samoa is communally owned.

Not surprisingly, there is pressure on Samoa's Government from outside moneylenders like the World Bank to change this. There are many foreign investors ready to help the Country develop, or more accurately, ready to exploit the wealth of Samoa's many assets for overseas corporate profit.

Thankfully, up to now this has been resisted by most Samoans. There are two universities in the Country of only 200,000 people. Many local leaders hold advanced degrees and doctorates from prestigious overseas universities. Because of its well-educated populace, the Country has managed to select the bits of Western civilization that suits it, like healthcare, education, religion and many material bits without giving up important parts of their own culture and way of life.

However, there are signs that this independence and uniqueness may not last. Under the terms and conditions of many loans and grants offered by the World Bank, the Chinese, Americans, Europeans and others, the moneylenders have been very subtly and patiently manipulating changes to local laws so future overseas corporate access will be easier. It may be only a matter of time before Samoa goes the way of the rest of the world.

The uniqueness of Samoa is not yet all gone, though. The most distinctive remaining aspect of traditional Samoan culture is its continued reliance on the use of consensus for most of its local public decision-making.

It is one of the few countries in the world that formally recognizes its value. It is even written into its Planning Act that one of the main functions of the body administering it is:

> *"To encourage the resolution of outcomes, disagreements and disputes arising from the operations of this Act by the reaching of consensus decisions;"* (English version)

To help local communities prepare their coastal management plans I sat in on more than 100 meetings with local communities around the country. Virtually all local level decision-making is still done by consensus, at least by the consensus of all heads of households, who are predominantly, but not entirely, male.

The Samoans with me did all the talking, primarily because it allowed the local community to discuss matters in their own language. Most Samoans know some English but my Samoan language skills are almost non-existent so I always had a translator beside me. Being there in person, however, let me observe first hand how consensus decision-making actually works in a country where it has been practiced for centuries.

Our first encounter with any community was always the most important. It began with an elaborate hour-long formal welcome. We could not arrive the first time without bringing our own Orator, or person of high status. Our Orator had to be able to trace a personal connection, usually ancestral, back to that community. Sometimes that linkage was tenuous, but it was important for the local people to know we actually had something in common with them.

Usually, all the household heads of the area were sitting down in the meeting hall when we arrived. Where they sat told us their relative importance in the community. The most important elder did not sit opposite the main entrance door where the chief executive in most Western offices or the priests in most churches would sit.

He sat against the wall (or posts if in an open-air building) on one side of the room flanked on either side by the other community members more or less in order of their status in the community. We were expected to sit against the wall opposite the local leaders with our most important people also sitting in the central spot among us.

Despite the clear recognition of an individual's importance, no one sat in a position of dominance. The more traditional meeting houses were round or oval so that everyone could sit in a circle equidistant from each other.

Unfortunately, the shape of newer meeting houses is slowly changing as cheap modern building practices tend to dictate rectangular structures, but even in the newest structures everyone still tries to sit in a circle facing each other rather than in rows facing toward the front.

The gathering always started with their local Orator and ours exchanging a few comments with each other. While this was happening, kava sticks from a number of local elders were gathered up and placed in front of our Orator. The most important visitor was then announced by name and title. Our Orator would examine the root balls on the sticks in front of him for their potential kava quality, and hand the best one to a younger member of the local community who in an exaggerated manner then pranced over to the head visitor and handed it to him or her. The next most important visitor was then similarly honored until our Orator ran out of local kava sticks.

While this was going on, at the side of the room opposite the door, a small group of young adults from the community, one usually an unmarried young woman, prepared the kava drink from powdered kava root and water.

Once the local kava sticks were distributed, it was loudly announced that the kava was ready to drink, and everyone in the room began to clap synchronously. This was followed by one of the young men near the kava bowl gracefully dipping a half coconut shell into the liquid, strutting across the floor with it and with a broad sweep handing it to the most important visitor.

He repeated the process with the most important local community leader, then the next most important visitor, and so on until everyone in the room had been served kava. After drinking the tea like, muddy colored, room temperature, bland tasting liquid, each recipient said a few words, mostly just thanks to God, although some said more personal or funny things.

It was a startlingly effective way for everyone in the room to understand who else was in the room with them. It clearly indicated how much respect each person had in his or her own community, before getting into the subject and the politics of the meeting itself.

The kava had an interesting effect as well. Only a small amount was drunk, but unlike the alcohol that some Westerners discretely use to help make decisions, the kava did not make people more self confident and aggressive. Its effects were slightly sedative, and instead seemed to contribute to the overall sense of peace and calmness at the meeting.

Usually the meeting began immediately after the kava ceremony, and lasted until everyone present had said everything he or she had wanted to say. The meeting ended with a full meal hosted by the local community, the giving of gifts to us, and us giving small gifts back to the local Orator, those running the kava ceremony and a few of the leading local elders, plus a much larger gift to the community as a whole.

All major gifts were loudly announced outside the meeting place by those who gave them so that everyone, particularly those not in attendance, would know about them.

Our gift to the community for the first meeting was invariably cash in small bills so it could be easily distributed among everyone there. It amounted to hundreds, even thousands of dollars depending on the number of people who attended the meeting, the quality of the meal and the gifts we received.

The community's gifts and our gifts seemed designed to show how much we valued each other, but also to subtly balance each other out. Just as the gifts and food from the community were raised from all the local people in accordance with what each could afford and their status in the community, what they each got back from us was usually related to both as well.

§

Apart from the kava ceremony and the encouragement

of a very full exchange of ideas, there were a number of other meticulously followed protocols for conducting Samoan meetings.

By far the most interesting to me was how local meetings considered opposing ideas. Outside the South Pacific, I have not seen anything like it. In virtually all other groups that I have worked with, if those making a decision encountered opposition, what they did next was very predictable.

If the opposing idea could not be incorporated into the current idea easily and at little cost, those leading the debate would check to see if they had a majority of supporters, and if they had, they would simply shut down the opposition as quickly as possible.

This would usually happen with a quick dismissive comment about the idea from someone in the majority group. If that didn't shut up the opponent, however, a more prolonged attack would be made on the idea itself, on the cost of it, or if neither of these were enough, on the character of the person or people putting forward the new idea.

Anyone who has ever been involved in a political debate knows this last stage of democratic decision-making can get very messy and destructive for all involved. Moreover, the final majority vote decision did not always end the matter. The closer the final vote was, the more extreme were the responses of both the winners and the losers. In any democracy with a free press (and no hidden junta), a close vote often just motivates the losers into louder and stronger opposition to try to keep the winners from picking up their prize. The winners then have to devote even more effort to obtain the benefits of their decision.

Samoan consensus decision-making worked in an entirely different way and resulted in a very different feeling at the end among all those involved.

When someone in a Samoan community raised an opposing idea to something that already seemed to have the backing of most at a meeting, the immediate response of everyone was attentive rather than dismissive.

The first thing that happened was someone supportive of the original idea would thank the "opponent" for bringing the alternative idea to the meeting's attention. He or someone else would then ask for more details about the new idea and what might make it better than the one already on the table.

The more radically different the new idea, the more attentive everyone was. The presenter was generally given whatever time he (or occasionally, she) felt was needed to explain the new idea and the reasoning behind it, and then the meeting would be opened up for discussion among all present.

Discussion was usually very polite as no one needed to be reminded that they all had to agree with the new idea, the opponent had to change his views to theirs, or they all had to find a mutually acceptable compromise if they wanted to proceed. The very nature of consensus decision-making made everyone involved think inclusively rather than divisively.

Debate between the opposing points of view could occasionally get very heated, however, and it was the role of both Orators to keep it respectful and on track at all times. The Orators generally did not participate in any of the debate, but if things got too tense, one of them would usually interject a joke to try to diffuse the tension. To play it safe, the joke was often directed at himself.

Invariably, the other Orator would then respond with a joke of his own until all in the meeting were chuckling to them selves if not laughing out loud. The Orator's interjections took only a minute or two. Once the tension was broken, more gentle debate quickly resumed.

Difficult debate could last for hours, but because everyone had to sit cross-legged on the floor while participating in the meeting, eventually tiredness set in. Anyone who has sat this way for a long period of time knows this is a very humbling position to maintain for more than an hour or two, particularly wearing the respectful Samoan skirt (all males) or puletasi dress (all females). This cleverly limits the overall length of any meeting. The growing stiffness and discomfort encourages everyone to find compromise so that they can stand up and stretch their legs.

Sometimes, though, the issues would be too contentious or complex to resolve in a single meeting. If that was the case, the meeting would then be adjourned so everyone could have time to think about the choices raised. Alternatively, all those at the meeting would agree on a small group of representatives to consider the alternatives. The small group would then meet later on their own to find a solution they thought everyone could live with.

§

Another thing that struck me about using consensus in a Samoan meeting was the main objective of everyone was not about getting unanimous support for some proposed idea or change. It was about appeasing any opposition to it.

The two objectives may sound the same but they are actually quite different. It is a little simplistic, but public support or opposition to any idea or change can usually be described as having the characteristics of a bell curve. That is, if a straight line were drawn on the ground through any group of people and the most extreme supporters of an idea were asked to stand at one end and its most extreme opponents at the other end, the vast majority of people would end up standing somewhere in the middle.

A long time observation of mine is that most people do not hold extreme views on everything. We may each have strong opinions about a few things, but most people cannot afford the time or the emotional energy to care strongly about every possible idea or change.

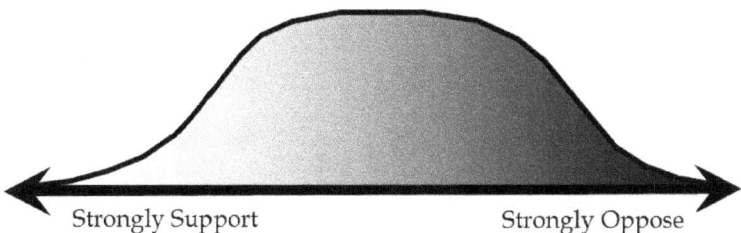

Strongly Support   Strongly Oppose

What has confirmed this to me over the years is the many dozens of community mail-back surveys I've personally undertaken on planning matters. They have all required local residents to answer a variety of questions on sometimes contentious planning issues before posting them back to the local Government.

For all surveys, the responses were tested after only a handful had arrived back, then again after most had been returned without prompting, and finally at the end following prolonged media harassment. One striking aspect of them all was that the results never depended on how interested people were in the subject.

Those that sent in their responses first were almost always the most interested. Yet their views were consistently no different (within a few percentage points on all questions) to the people who sent in their survey forms last.

The surveys showed me that for some people their strongest interests were personal, related to their own health, comfort, wealth or power. For others their strongest interests were communal; about social justice, peace and the environment. Yet among both types of interests, any given individual seemed to be able to focus only on what he or she thought they could realistically affect.

In normal majority vote democratic decision-making, most effort is focused on shifting the line through the large, most disinterested part of the group so that the bulge of people is slightly bigger on one side than on the other.

To do this requires first waking up the most disinterested people in any group with exaggerated, often very inaccurate claims about the losses or gains that will happen if the change occurs.

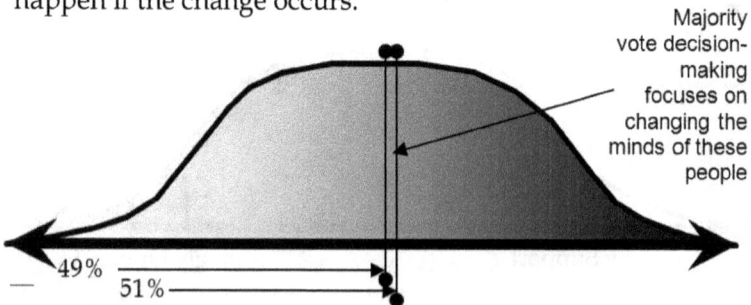

Majority vote decision-making focuses on changing the minds of these people

49%

51%

To do this requires first waking up the most disinterested people in any group with exaggerated, often very inaccurate claims about the losses or gains that will happen if the change occurs.

Such exaggerated claims work well with a free press where polarized debate is commercially profitable. The right to a free press is written into most country's constitutions supposedly to ensure all views are heard, but the reality is, there is a symbiotic relationship between democratic debate and privately owned news media. The driving force behind any free press is controversy. Polarized debate, the kind that majority vote based democracies require, sells news.

It is ironic that the current amalgamation of private media ownership and the homogenization of media content around the world could be killing both the free press and democracy.

Throughout many countries today, private newspapers and television stations are running into difficulties. Some blame it on the internet, and there is probably some truth to this. However, it is not difficult to see at the same time that this important, commercially motivated check on democratic decision-making may also be growing weaker because corporate sponsors (the advertisers who pay for it) are owned and managed by fewer and fewer diverse interests.

Under consensus decision-making, such limitations of privately owned media are not important. Solutions that involve extreme views are rarely approved. If the merits of an extreme view (on either side) become obvious, they will be taken on board by everyone in the group and then obviously, they are no longer extreme. However, if they remain extreme to most everyone, they eventually just fade away.

They fade away because without the win-lose motivation of majority vote decision-making, when no one else likes an extreme idea after it has been fully discussed, those holding them eventually accept that it isn't worth pursuing the matter any further.

It doesn't mean that those holding the extreme views come to agree with everyone else, only that to preserve their own ability to participate in future decisions and live happily with everyone else, they eventually choose not to continue pushing their ideas when it becomes clear most people simply don't agree with them.

Depending on the divisiveness of the issue and the emotional trauma encountered in the discussions, a group decision may require up to 95% support to achieve consensus.

However, a decision made by consensus almost never requires unanimous support. In fact, I have witnessed rare occasions when it does not even require the support of a majority of those present.

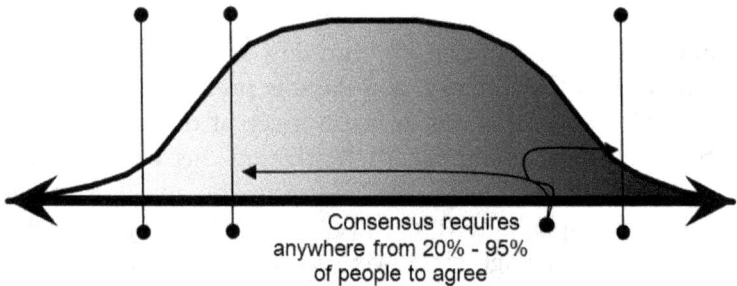

Consensus requires anywhere from 20% - 95% of people to agree

If some members of a group are adamantly in favor of a particular decision and the rest, while not supportive of it, don't strongly oppose it, just 20%-30% of those present can achieve a group decision favorable to them by consensus.

Simply by not continuing debate on an opposing idea it quickly becomes clear to the others present that the matter is no longer an issue.

There is no vote taken.

Former opponents do not have to pledge their loyalty to everyone else. There is no exaggerated elation at the "win" either, just a renewed sense of community and peace among everyone present, including with the former "opponents".

Of course, the social pressure on those with unsupported ideas to capitulate in the face of extreme isolation is itself a potential problem. Some have described the Samoan culture as "the great clobbering machine" to creative thinking. Those bucking the norm can experience severe social pressure. In some cases, radically different ideas have led to people being permanently banished from their own communities. I have heard stories of Samoans who left the country altogether rather than conform to such pressure. However, for the vast majority of Samoans, this does not seem to be a problem.

Personally, I believe there is a role for social pressure in society if its "clobbering" nature can be minimized. Western society's current emphasis on individual freedom and the "me, myself and I" syndrome could be contributing to many of the social problems that face our planet today. A little social pressure on those severely narcissistic or socially inconsiderate might do us all some good.

§

One of the most significant outcomes of Samoan Consensus Decision-making came as a surprise to me. I did not discover it until near the end of my work there.

From my experience, a land use plan for a large town can take up to five years to finalize even under the best planning legislation; one to three years of community input to develop it, plus at least the same amount of time wrangling in the courts over some of the details before its formal adoption. By then some parts of it are often out of date. Nevertheless, because of the difficulties getting the plan to that point, it is put into operation despite its growing irrelevance.

With consensus decision-making, there is virtually no delay in finalizing plans or seeing them implemented once everyone agrees to them. The initial phases in the development of the coastal plans in Samoa did not always run smoothly, but once completed the plans were finalized and signed off almost immediately.

As a result, the time and costs spent on the overall planning process was often actually less than what would have been spent in most other countries undertaking similar planning work under similar legislation, but not using consensus.

Admittedly, Samoa is a unique case. Communal land ownership and the Country's long history of consensus decision-making do make a difference. However, for me, the simplicity of adopting a plan formulated through the consensus process was quite extraordinary to witness.

Chapter 7:

The Key: *describes how consensus decision-making could be made to work in groups involving thousands, even billions of people by using a simple "linked" multi-level structure of decision-making.*

Most ways to make public decisions have their down sides.

- Wars kill people. They also cost a great deal of public money.
- The market place is good at achieving efficient outcomes, but it is often at the expense of social cooperation and a sustainable environment.
- Dictatorships and monarchies, even those run by benevolent dictators, are particularly subject to the whims of a few.
- Democracies rarely meet the needs of minority groups, and can severely polarize people.
- Consensus decision-making does not work in large groups, particularly if they contain narcissists

While no method of making public decisions is without its drawbacks, there is only one, consensus decision-making, that can consistently consider the interests of everyone involved, not just the most powerful, rich or numerous. It is also the only one that can reach decisions that consistently result in peaceful and publicly accepted outcomes for all involved.

Consensus decision-making does not require the rich giving gifts to the poor to keep them quiet or the majority telling minorities what is really good for them. It is not an ignorant indulgence of power over the powerless. Instead, it is the only method of decision-making that virtually removes the use of power from the process of decision-making altogether. It literally takes the questions of "Who's the strongest?", "Who's got the money?" and "Who knows best?" out of the equation.

Its only real drawback is that it does not work in large groups. But this does not mean that consensus is an unrealistic way for modern societies to make public decisions. Consensus decision-making in public jury trials has been used in some nations for centuries. A few town meetings in New England, the Society of Friends (Quakers) worldwide and many peace-oriented groups now use it.

Even decision makers at the highest levels of NATO and the United Nations use it to reach their most important decisions. The media often put this last example in a negative light by complaining that one of the "Big five" members of the United Nations Security Council has "vetoed" a desired action. Because all five permanent members of the Security Council must reach decisions by consensus, if one of them dislikes what the others want to do, one vote can stop any action the UN as a whole might want to take.

Rather than being negative, the use of consensus at the highest level of the UN generally ensures that a single country cannot become the ultimate power broker.

Rissia's invasion of The Ukraine, however, shows there is a downside to even the use of consensus in some circumstances. It assumes no country would ever be willing to threaten nuclear annihilation to get their way, as Russia's leader Vladimir Putin has.

§

Faced with the obvious group size limitation of consensus decision-making, years ago I began to look for alternative ways to use it. I was convinced that there could be a way to unlock its potential; some sort of key that would allow its use in public decision-making despite its inability to involve large numbers of people.

I did not have to look very long or hard to find it.

Our armies now use a system of decision-making that shows how it could work. Although our military institutions are probably the worst example I could use because of their purpose and the regimented unquestioned authoritarianism inherent in them, they all use a hierarchical or pyramid style of organization that allows communication from top commanders to be sent very quickly and efficiently to large numbers of soldiers in the field through a number of intermediate levels of command. Significantly, they also allow similarly speedy communication between levels in the opposite direction.

It is strange, given this characteristic, that they are not used in more peaceful applications, such as in the decision-making of Quakers and Green Party members.

§

Most government institutions are already organized in a potentially similar way, although this is not generally obvious and their inter-level communication is often non-existent. Our health systems, education systems, legal systems and political systems, for instance, all use some form of hierarchical structure to manage their affairs.

The "soldier in the field" level of our health system is ourselves. When we get sick, we go to bed and rest. The next level up is our family to whom we turn for help if we cannot get well by ourselves. Then we might go to a local shop for a home remedy or "over the counter" medicine to treat our ailment.

For more severe health matters, we might seek the advice of a neighborhood doctor or pharmacist. Another "level" up, when the skills of an individual medical practitioner are not enough, we would go to a city clinic or a small hospital, and finally as a last resort, we might seek a national or even international medical facility to help us solve a particularly major, unusual or specialist health problem. Therefore, at the moment in most countries if we get sick there are at least five or six "levels" of medical institutions available to us.

Another example of an existing hierarchy of sorts is our education system. Parents, mostly mothers in western households, lead the education system on the first level, although in some cultures such input is supplemented by fathers, grandparents and extended family members. A second level is often introduced through playmates and siblings. A third level comes with the introduction of formal teaching, often beginning with child care facilities and kindergartens, followed by a fourth level found in primary school grades 1- 6 and a fifth in secondary school grades 7-12, or their equivalents. Then comes tertiary level education and post graduate level education, followed finally by "on the job" apprenticeships, or what amounts to a 6 or 7th level of one on one personal instruction.

Probably the best example of an existing multi-leveled hierarchy is our current democratic governments. Those decision-making structures controlling what an individual does with his or her life starts with an individual's own conscience. This is tempered by his or her family and the household he or she lives in, then by a community or clan council (where there is one), then by a city (urban) or county (rural) council, then by a regional authority if the area governed is very large, then by a state or provincial government, then by a country's government, then by the General Assembly of the United Nations, and finally by its Security Council. Depending on exactly where someone lives there can be as few as six to as many as a dozen levels of government decision-making controlling our own actions and those of everyone else on this planet.

§

The significance of this multi-leveled structure found in most of our existing institutions is that this structure could actually be used to facilitate the use of consensus decision-making.

Most democracies have discovered that even they

cannot make decisions with very large numbers of politicians involved, even after painting all choices in black and white. Chambers of parliament or congress around the world invariably contain less than 1000 members. Even those with only half that number are often mired in chaos at times.

If such groups of political decision-makers were instead limited to just 20 people, making decisions together by consensus might not be easy, but it certainly would not be impossible.

If a family or a group of people living together in one household could choose one representative from among themselves to look after their interests, and then if twenty of those "household representatives" chose by consensus one among them to represent their interests on a second level of governance, and then if twenty of those representatives did the same on a third level and so on, it would only take seven levels of "consensus government" to run the entire planet.

That is, under a government hierarchy that used consensus decision-making with just 20 people in any decision-making group, there could actually be fewer levels of government controlling people's lives on this planet than now exist in many parts of the world.

Even more significantly, on every level of government in such a consensus based structure, those individuals representing groups of people would be personally known to every person involved in their selection. Because there would only be 20 people involved in any decision, all those involved would know the personality, the knowledge and the true expertise of the person they were choosing to represent them.

Today under our current democratically elected government systems, almost no voter can claim such knowledge. For most voters, any knowledge they may have about their representative, if it could be called knowledge, is only gained through the often exaggerated, sales driven hype or bought political advertisements in the media by professional "spin doctors".

In a multi-leveled consensus based system there would

be almost no opportunity for fake news or biased reporting to affect group decisions. There would be almost no opportunity for narcissists to buy their own selection as representatives, either.

If the size of consensus decision-making groups were kept down to around ten people in each of them, consensus would be even easier to achieve. Yet with only ten people in every group, it would require just ten "levels" of government to run the entire world. (10^{10} = ten billion people). This is still fewer levels of government than found in some of the more developed, populated parts of the world today.

This description about the number of levels needed to run a global government is actually a "worst case scenario" too. It assumes that everyone, everywhere will always want to be involved in their own governance. At least half won't because of their age. Voting age in most countries is now at least 18 and while voter turn out may be high for the elderly, for the young it is often less than half those eligible.

I also wouldn't expect every household to be represented in the lowest level group either; only those which:

> 1. Had a member with a strong desire to participate in their own governance, or
> 2. Had a particular grievance they wanted to resolve.

I would imagine most people would not bother to get involved once the initial dust settled down and people realized just how well their personal interests were met by a consensus based government that ensured consideration of all interests, including minority interests, equally.

With such a multi-leveled, structured way to make group decisions it would be possible to make even global decisions without having to invent radically new forms of government institutions.

This is profoundly important because if all existing

levels of decision-making now found in our public health, education and other similar institutions could be re-aligned to fit into the various levels of a consensus-based hierarchy or "structure" of government, theoretically all public decision-making could be integrated together across all existing institutions.

The remainder of this book starts again from the beginning of the global puzzle, only this time accepting that the use of "structured consensus decision-making" as I call it, might be possible if we were willing to modify our existing institutions a little to allow this to happen.

Chapter 8:

In Search of the "Big Picture": *tries to make sense of the incredible complexity of today's world. Eventually five significant pieces of the puzzle are uncovered involving Personal, Economic, Equity, Community and Environmental change.*

When my wife and I moved to Philadelphia from New Zealand in the late 1990s we lived right in the downtown on a ginkgo tree lined cobblestone alley in a charming 3-story historic brick cottage. We had wonderful warm friendly neighbors. It genuinely felt like the perfect place to live, with friends, shops, theatres and work all within a few blocks of our doorstep.

However, daily, when I stepped out of our Shangri-La to be a planner in the real world, I had to walk around the beggars lying in the city's main streets and pretend they did not exist.

My actions reminded me of Colin Turnbull's study of the Ik mountain people in Uganda 35 years earlier. Such indifference to serious human need, he had concluded, was one of the end stages of a dying society.

It made me wonder if everyone in the world today who walks around strangers lying in the street has learned how to turn off his/her social conscience like the Ik did during the deadly famine in their homeland in the 1960s.

The problem is particularly obvious in the USA where the surrounding wealth highlights the difference between those with money and those without, but Americans are certainly not the only people to have learned how to block out their consciences to the plight of others. Today, large parts of the planet have learned how to do the same.

I suspect Colin Turnbull would blame the global loss of

compassion on the human instinct to survive in hard times whatever the cost. In my more pessimistic moments, I am hard pressed not to agree with him. The outlook for humanity does seem rather grim at times.

However, even in the back woods of Southwest Ethiopia not far away in time or place from where Mr. Turnbull studied the Ik people, I never saw anyone so desperate that they ignored their neighbors. Most of the people living in absolute poverty in the remote village of grass huts where my wife and I lived still would stop to give their last ear of corn to help another person.

It made me think that perhaps there are other things going on when we walk around the beggars in the street; that our growing lack of empathy may have other causes besides simply wanting to survive in hard times.

One of the reasons for our changing empathy, I believe, could be that we are no longer able to see the "big picture" and our place on this planet. We have become so self-focused and life has become so complex that it is impossible for most people to understand how their own life is related to the homeless person in the street. We can see no reason why we should help him, much less, how we could help him in any meaningful way.

Because of the complexity of the world today, I think most people now choose to let their governments sort out their less personal relationships with others. We hope that our vote for president or for our congressional representative will ensure the right thing is done for the other guy.

However, try talking with any politician anywhere about it and you will quickly discover that even the best ones have little time to look at the big picture. They are invariably rushed off their feet trying hard to solve just one or two problems they think they might have a chance to fix, not all of them.

Admittedly, it is not hard to find a bad politician and think they must all be bad, but for the most part the politicians themselves are not the problem. Of the many hundreds that I have worked with during my career, I have found very few in it solely for the money or power.

Most politicians really seem to have a genuine social conscience and want to help improve the world. It is just that most also have to scale the seriously corrupting wall of election finance to participate in the process. Alternatively, they are already rich and have been taught to believe that paternalism is a gift they can give others, or possibly an obligation to uphold, but certainly not a serious political liability.

The scary part is that if our politicians do not have the time or resources to step back and take a holistic view of what is going on in the world around them, who else does? All of our other institutions have had to gear themselves toward problem solving one at a time because, like our politicians, no institutional administrator or board of directors can afford the time or resources to see how any change they might introduce could affect the operation of another institution somewhere else. They are all market driven and judged almost entirely by economic indicators.

There are, of course, a myriad of special interest groups willing and able to do this. It is no surprise that a large amount of public money goes into defense budgets, insurance programs, financial institutions and other private corporations because they have the money and time to look at the big picture and ensure at least their own futures are secure.

Universities once tried to give tertiary students a global perspective; a holistic view of the world, too. The very word university comes from this intent. However, nowadays none of them can afford such luxury. Under the demands of a market place led society, university students today must focus on a career that will allow them to survive in the world as it is. University output and their level of success in education is now measured by their students' employability in the market place not by their students' understanding of life and the world around them.

§

The market place has a lot to answer for, for making our world so complex, but the reason for the world's current chaos is not just related to how we now handle money. The cause is much bigger than that.

When there were only a few people on this earth, the clearance of a new field, someone's move to a new place or the accidental death of a friend was no reason to start a world war. Although such changes sometimes caused conflict, the problems were local and could be quickly resolved by those directly involved. However, as humans evolved and increased in numbers, the pace of change and the potential for conflict between people also increased.

Consequently, over the last few millennia as community populations have grown from just a few dozen people to many millions, people have invented a number of "systems" to help them deal with the ever-increasing complexity and stress in their lives caused by such change.

To make life easier, safer and more understandable, humans have developed political systems, religious systems, economic systems, defense systems, judicial systems, education systems, health systems, child rearing systems, amusement systems, transportation systems, communication systems, and more recently, environmental management systems, among a thousand others.

Once established, each of these "systems" has continued to evolve through interaction with other systems and with our ever changing technology and environment to the point where today it is hard to tell just what systems there are in operation around the world and what each is trying to do, where, how and to whom.

In addition, while each of these "systems" involves some physical and/or financial resource, it is now often extremely difficult to tell just what resources are involved, and who, if anyone, is responsible for them.

The way the term "system" is used here is similar to, but not the same as how Biologist Ludwig Von Bertalanffy used the term for his "System's Theory" back in the 1940s. He used the term "system" to describe the multiplying effect of interlinked change on the whole, while my use of the term here simply describes any process that includes or results in change. The reason for clarifying this is that unless the change involves only natural resources, it is important to note that there is always some form of human involvement in it; that is, some form of active or passive human decision-making.

§

Our invention of political systems is a case in point. All of our present political systems probably started innocently enough. It isn't too difficult to imagine a group of villagers turning to a wise village elder for advice when drought caused local crops to fail, or when a hunting party inadvertently killed a pet dik dik.

At some very distant point in the past, however, it is clear that some of the wise elders started to see their advice for what it was worth: power and wealth. They started to call themselves medicine men, chiefs and kings and to take formal control, first by friendly persuasion and then by force.

It isn't clear whether this new political arrangement was responsible for speeding up technological development or whether it was the other way around, but what is clear is that as technology improved, peoples' access to advice, and thus to their own ability to solve problems and reduce stress in their lives improved too. People began to recognize that they could have their own power and wealth if they took charge themselves. So beginning a few thousand years ago some of the people who had lost political control, decided to take it back again.

The limited democracies of Greece in the 5th century BC were the earliest fully documented attempts, then San Marino (4th century AD), the Isle of Man (10th century) and a few others resurrected the idea quite a bit later, but it was the English's adoption into law of the Magna Carta in 1297 that finally got the idea firmly entrenched as a system option. Seven centuries of refinement followed, with notable strides being made with the ideas of Lock, Montesquieu and others during the 17th, 18th and 19th centuries.

In the 19th and 20th centuries, Communism and Socialism attempted to take humanity even further down the track of social responsibility in government by trying to bring under political control the omnipotent ideology of the market place.

Most Communists, however, eventually had to give up

their fight over this passion of Marx after mortgaging themselves to Western technology.

In the last few decades many socialist countries, including Great Britain, Sweden and New Zealand have also had to alter their social justice programs, sometimes radically, after global competition and the threat of being left behind forced them to tighten up on how they spent their profits.

With the dispassionate support of the market place, however, technological development has not been similarly bridled. It has raced ahead while social development has struggled to keep hold of what was gained a hundred years ago.

In the first two decades of the Twenty First Century, the death and destruction of the wars in Syria, Afghanistan, Iraq, and Palestine like the death and destruction of World War I, World War II, the Vietnam War and the Korean War in the Twentieth Century yet again drew public attention to our present developmental imbalance.

Today, there are few who don't believe we will see more damning proof of this imbalance, possibly even our own extinction as a species through a nuclear or solar induced global melt-down, unless something serious is done to address the problem peacefully.

§

There are at least two reasons for such pessimism. The obvious one is the problem of global space. This small planet has simply become too populated and technologically far too complex for the old systems to work effectively any more.

Our old, relatively primitive institutions were never designed to work with such sophisticated tools within such an intensely used environment. They were never designed to operate under the extreme lifestyles that now exist between the haves and the have-nots. Space is no longer infinite and can no longer hide the inequities.

Every culture has its own unique mixture of locally created systems to meet its needs. Some locally developed systems would work well anywhere and are easily transported to other cultures, but some are not. As a result every culture has its strong and weak features, depending on which systems happen to evolve or get introduced in a particular way, to a particular environment, among a particular group of people, at a particular point in time.

Today, there is no longer room to have any buffer space between groups of people using different mixtures of systems. The people in castles can no longer hide behind high walls or deep forests. Now everyone is tripping over each other. Some systems that worked well enough within one group are now found intermingled with the systems of other groups and causing mayhem far from their origin.

The strife this sometimes causes is not a new phenomenon, but it is certainly increasing in frequency and intensity. Even in the early stages of civilization, when small groups of people moved into an area that was already using its resources to capacity and could not easily handle more people, the original occupants of the area invariably turned racist or fascist to protect what they had.

When large groups moved into less populated areas, the new residents almost always systematically marginalized, converted or exterminated the existing people just to ensure continued social harmony among themselves.

Nowadays, there is an even more frightening phenomenon. In addition to the continuing problems of cultural racism and marginalization that occur when there is migration from one area to another, when large numbers of people now move into large urban areas, whole social systems can virtually disappear overnight. The result is the creation of urban ghettos governed by little more than the power of the gun.

Unfortunately, given the fixed and finite amount of space on this planet, the rapid depletion of global resources and the likelihood of continued population growth for some time yet, the problems created by intermingling incompatible systems from different cultures are not likely to get better, only worse.

§

The other reason for believing the end of humanity could be near is that war and its symbiotic partner, the market place, are increasingly being used by our governments as the way to resolve the problems caused by our rising population, diminishing resources and finite space, but history has shown neither can do this.

As Jesus, Mohammed and virtually all past prophets around the planet understood, and many historians convincingly argue today, neither war nor the market place is capable of solving the many major problems that face our planet.

Yet war and the market place continue to be held up by our governments as the best ways to solve our problems. They are sold like LOTTO tickets to the poor and to others who feel they have no alternative options in life.

To those individuals who have nowhere else to turn, the financial rewards that playing soldier can offer. can be very appealing. For the planet as a whole, however, men with guns court disaster. Those who bought or made the guns then need to justify their purchase or business by finding wars to fight.

To the world, capitalism is held out as the golden chalice for all. "Just work hard and you too will win," those getting rich in it say, knowing that this is an absurdity. Under pure capitalism there are no winners unless there are also many more losers.

If left unbridled, the market place inevitably creates ever-growing disparities between those who have everything and those who have nothing which equally inevitably, leads to further and ever-more catastrophic war to try to readjust the imbalance.

Up until thirty years ago, many Westerners were fearfully aware of Marx's vision of the ending of the market place and are now relieved that its corruption in the form of Communism has largely failed.

However, Marx's vision of a social uprising by the proletariat seems only a minor consequence of the problems the planet faces today. With the massive stockpile of nuclear weapons at our fingertips, relentless global warming, out of control population growth, serious global inequities and no real clue how to fix the mess we're in, it doesn't take a visionary to see how this could end.

§

All of the planet's current institutions including all our governments and religions are specifically set up to be self-perpetuating; that is, they are all designed to keep going regardless of what happens around them. In the past, this was one of their most important characteristics. Today, however, their self-perpetuation is leading us all like lemmings over a cliff because none of them are programmed to self-correct when faced with the imminent demise of humanity.

Even the American Government, once praised for its ability to "self correct" and recover from complex problems, is a good example of this, although most governments today suffer from similar problems.

It is true that the French philosopher Montesquieu's three part form of government with its legislative, executive and judicial "checks and balances" has helped. America's democracy has survived for nearly 250 years, a bit longer than the democracy of Athens. It has also earned top marks for helping the world follow a better path through the last two centuries than many of the paths the planet could have followed.

However, America's current government structure, most particularly its Constitution, part of its "judicial" check, has a number of potentially fatal flaws that its founding fathers could never have foreseen.

One of them is the Constitution's single-minded focus on the rights of the individual over all other rights. No one could have foreseen the power of the market place subtly usurping the collective consciences of people and the social fabric of their communities.

If individual rights remain the only thing that matters in the USA and corporations continue to be considered "individuals" there, as resources grow scarce, under the leveling forces of the market place and the US Constitution, people in the US will eventually be forced to give away their own morals to financially compete with them.

US corporations haven't had any morals since they were

allowed to drop their original legal moral requirement to serve the public interest more than 100 years ago. Corporations can now focus entirely on the bottom line of profit. Individuals may eventually have to do the same unless there is some legal recognition of the value of morals and social justice inserted into America's founding document.

Another fatal flaw of the US Government is its reliance on private media to tell the public the full story about what big government and big business are really doing to them. In 1776, no one could have foreseen almost all of the major media being bought up by just a few corporations with little interest in giving the public the full picture of what is happening around them.

Private media has grown very sophisticated in downplaying or ignoring the half of the news they don't want people to hear. Even public radio and television, such as they are in America and other countries, often have to negotiate corporate dogma and finance to survive.

The internet, once thought to be the public's savior as the way to overcome the growing corruption of the media, has so far proven unable to do this. In fact, fake news on the internet is now virtually impossible to detect. Even worse, the deceptive tools now used there are increasingly being picked up and redistributed by the main media as real news.

A third potentially fatal flaw was mentioned at the beginning of Chapter 3; the "Eisenhower Prophesy". Who could have foreseen Congress, the Military and major private Industry all in bed together lining their own pockets at the public's expense? Each one now supports the other in a circular mutually beneficial relationship that has no reason what-so-ever to change.

§

Perhaps though, the American Constitution's largest potentially fatal flaw and the Country's greatest vulnerability is its reliance on the market place to choose who runs the County.

Back when the Bill of Rights was being drafted, there was concern over the possibility that one person might have to represent the interests of 30,000 people. The worst-case scenario they could imagine was one representative per 50,000. That's a large town. They were fearful that even with the help of the media, voters could never fully understand who they were voting for.

Today in the US Congress, one representative on average looks after the interests of over 700,000 people. That's almost fifteen times the original worst vision of the Constitution's authors. In the US Senate, just one person can now represent up to 20 million people.

At one to thirty thousand, there was a remote possibility that at least some voters would know a little about the real person they were voting for, but today there is almost no chance of this in major elections.

What the public knows about any politician is almost entirely from what that politician has paid advertisers to tell them. It is not surprising why so many of our politicians are either very rich or start off as actors.

§

Part of the reason why I became disillusioned with American politics 45 years ago was an election that was held in Colorado back in the mid 1970s while I was a planner for a small city there. It was just after new national legislation had been passed to control election finance reporting in American politics, and it was still relatively free of loopholes.

The local newspaper published what all candidates had spent on their own election and the number of votes they had each received. Of the forty or so candidates that had run for office, there was an almost perfect correlation between the amount they had each spent on their campaigns and the number of votes they had each received. The lesson back then was clear and simple: Money buys votes.

Despite multiple attempts over the last 200 years to try to limit the domination of the rich (including corporations) in US elections, nothing has changed much today. In fact in 2010 the US Supreme Court ruled that corporations were indeed just like individuals when it came to election finances and were no longer banned (since 2002) from promoting candidates that supported their interests.

§

An example of the market place's effect on voting, judging from the many internet articles on the subject, is the many people both inside and outside the US who believe that the hundreds of thousands of deaths in Iraq from the Gulf Wars is a simple example of the corporate morals (or the lack of them) now endemic in US Government decision-making.

I suspect history will show that Robert Fisk and other correspondents covering the Iraq war were right; that the US invaded Iraq not as retribution over the Trade Tower attacks or because Saddam Hussein was hiding "weapons of mass destruction", but because Iraq had one of the largest untapped oil deposits in the world and the US wanted to control it.

Earlier, Iraq had changed all its oil contracts from US dollars to Euro dollars and the financial return they were then getting was encouraging other countries to consider re-negotiating their oil contracts into Euro Dollars as well.

Had the idea caught on, the value of the US dollar might well have plummeted on world markets because its value is largely stabilized by its use as the international currency of choice for buying and selling oil. One of the first things the US did on gaining control over Iraq was to change its oil contracts back to US dollars.

Many hope that the US can become a social and spiritual leader of the planet again, but I think the Country will have to introduce at least four changes to its Constitution before it might regain its former credibility in the world. They include:

- Introducing election finance reform that strictly limits election spending and cannot be circumvented;
- Clarifying the rights of individuals to exclude corporations,
- Including community rights, and
- Establishing a free and independent, publicly funded news media accessible to all covering, radio, television, and the internet.

§

Unfortunately, even if all of these things were included in amendments to the American Constitution, there would still be no guarantee that the planet would be better off for it. The likelihood would certainly increase significantly, but the problems that the planet now faces are much greater than those attributable to any one country, even the USA.

The main problem facing us all is that there is now no obvious comprehensive way for the world to fix or even just manage the complexity of the mess it is in. Thank goodness for the United Nations and its vision of the future or I don't think we'd have made it even this far. However, as a long-term means of bringing peace to this planet, like all other existing governments, it is also fatally flawed by its structure.

It is helpful that the UN's power is controlled collectively by five major countries, not just by one of them. But it still relies most of the time on majority vote decision-making, which ensures the weaker or smaller minorities are largely ignored. Without serious structural changes at the UN to increase its use of consensus decision-making, we may all still end up the proverbial creek without a paddle.

It isn't necessarily all doom and gloom, though. Speeding up both the demise of humanity and its possible salvation, is improved global communication and education. Despite its limitations, the internet and other electronic media now allow an increasingly large percentage of the world to see and understand what our present paternalistic governments and public institutions are doing to us. With awareness and knowledge can come solutions.

Many people are working on them. Some have been for decades. My favorites include the authors Dennis Meadows, Mark Morford, Noam Chomsky, John Buck, and musicians Pete Seeger and Harry Chapin.

§

Looking for solutions to global problems has been an interest of mine for a long time too. However, for many years what stopped me from pursuing my passion, apart from needing to earn a living to support my family, was that I just could not find any way to begin to describe all the problems we faced, much less understand how they might be collectively resolved.

As you've just discovered reading the jumbled collection of thoughts contained in this chapter, there is no easy way to identify the planets problems, much less uncover how they might be fixed. Each problem seems to be inextricably entwined with many others like the contents of a juicer with fruit, vegetables and meat blended together on high. No matter what order these items are added, both the detail and the "big picture" always come out looking like thick, gross, indefinable brown pulp.

§

To find a way to describe the real concoction of our currently blended planetary chaos, several decades ago I began to examine existing library classification systems, like the Dewey Decimal Classification System, the Library of Congress Classification system and the Colon Classification System to see how they looked at the world. Libraries around the globe have struggled to find a logical way to organize human knowledge for several millennia.

I spent a long time trying to use or modify them to help me in my search, but was ultimately forced to conclude that none of them would ever be able to classify the information needed for good governance in a simple and easily accessible way.

What was needed was not yet another way to classify all knowledge. What was needed was a way to classify all "systems".

During this time it slowly became clear to me that good government is about handling "systems", or types of change, well; about managing or influencing the introduction, monitoring, stabilizing, enforcing, altering or stopping change.

So I started to look at the problems that we all now face on this planet in terms of "systems" of change. By shuffling and reshuffling lists of both local and global problems, eventually a way to describe almost all of them emerged out of the chaos. Although arguably overly simplistic, I think it is possible to describe all our problems as involving one or more of only five types of systems of change. These systems are:

- Personal systems
- Economic systems
- Equity systems
- Community systems
- Environmental systems

Personal Systems are those systems that are unique to an individual and arise from the actions of a person's own body, mind, character, experience and response to the environment around him or her. Such systems include those involving the consumption of food, the occupation of shelter, the establishment and maintenance of friendships, the procreation and nurturing of children, the ownership of physical and intellectual property, the pursuit of pleasure and happiness, the feeling and expression of emotions, and the perception of the five bodily senses. By definition, however, they do not include Economic and Equity systems, as described below

Economic Systems are those systems that involve the private transfer of resources between systems. The private transfer of resources can occur through resource use, work, sales or other forms of private exchange and is identified by a change in ownership or value. Such activities as banking, administration, professional services, personal services, trade (including barter), industry, construction, mining and commercial agriculture are all economic systems.

Equity Systems are systems designed to ensure fairness, impartiality and justice in any change involving human decision-making. The term, as used here, is not a technical reference to the residual value of encumbered property, the term's other meaning. The primary purpose of Equity Systems is to maintain independent public control over the relationships that other systems have with each other. They include our political systems, tax systems, planning & evaluation systems, weights and measures systems, defense systems, police systems, legal systems, punishment systems and public records systems, among others.

Community Systems are those systems that involve collective human responses to the environment. In general, they are larger public versions of personal systems but, like Personal Systems, by definition do not include either Economic or Equity systems. Community Systems include public media systems, public health systems, public education systems, religious systems, cultural heritage systems, public recreation systems, and social support systems like disability and unemployment benefits, public health insurance, public housing and retirement schemes.

Finally, Environmental Systems provide the physical setting that allows each of us to exist. They are essentially the various "eco" systems found on our globe, whether or not they contain humans or have been modified by them. They include all systems involving natural resources such as land, water, minerals, air, energy, plants and animals (including humans), plus all movement systems and systems involving the physical or technological improvements added by humans such as buildings and roads, that is, the physical attributes of civilization.

There are a few systems that are difficult to compartmentalize into one of these five types, but this does not really matter. The classification of systems into a handful of types is just a way to make thinking about them easier, and any system included in one category can easily be shifted to another if it makes thinking about it easier for a group of people.

Interestingly, however, the juxtaposition of these five types of systems provides similar benefits to those provided in current democratic forms of government by Montesquieu's well-tested theory of balancing power by separating executive, legislative and judicial functions.

The five types of systems described above have a similar in-built stabilizing mechanism when collectively introduced into consensus decision-making. Like executive, legislative and judicial powers, each of these five types of systems has unique interests to counter-balance the powers of the other four.

Self-interest is the most obvious and significant power behind Personal Systems, but the natural tendency for humans to be gregarious is an obvious and significant counter balancing drive behind Community Systems.

The drive for short-term efficiency in Economic Systems is similarly counter-balanced by every person's desire for long-term security, the primary focus of Equity Systems. And as Montesquieu partially understood even back in the early 1700s, the fifth set of systems, Environmental Systems provides its own balance if given the chance, for it is an important fixed determinant of the other four.

There is an acronym that makes it easy to remember these five types of systems. It's PEECE.

Reality, as opposed to theory, of course, is not quite as simple (or badly spelled) as this. However, this hypothesis has helped me construct a way to identify and clarify the very complex problems now faced by our existing democratic institutions.

Chapter 9:

So Where Should We Be Headed?

looks at all the goals that various religions, cultures and governments have set out for people to live by over the last several millennia starting with Moses, Siddhartha Gautama and Confucius.

Many people over the course of human history have tried to identify what the overall goals for humanity ought to be. The existence of written rules for people to live by goes back at least a thousand years before Moses was given God's "Ten Commandments" around 1300 BC. Among others, both the Egyptian ruler, Ptahhotep in 2450 BC and the Babylonian King, Hammurabi in 1750 BC, introduced long lists of rules to ensure consistent justice for their subjects. But the Ten Commandments were the first to receive geographically widespread and prolonged, non-political publicity.

The Bible tries to explain why they were introduced, but it is difficult to believe that it was all just about convincing people there was only one God. Possibly the bigger picture was that they may have been intended to help a large group of people under stress create social harmony and some sense of unity among themselves.

The last seven are relevant in any discussion of goals for humanity, regardless of one's religious persuasion:

1. You shall rest one day in seven,

2. You shall honor your father and mother,

3. You shall not murder,

4. You shall not commit adultery,

5. You shall not steal,

6. You shall not lie,

7. You shall not covet your neighbor's house, wife, slaves, etc.

In China seven or eight centuries later, Confucius included in his teachings the idea of empathetic reciprocity; that is, the idea of treating others the way you'd like to be treated yourself. He wasn't religious. Using ancient texts as a guide, he was interested in how to maintain social order and ensure good governance. He didn't consider everyone except friends as equals but did recognise that each person had his or her own place in society and should accept it.

Moses had introduced the idea of empathetic reciprocity much earlier than this as an adjunct to his ten commandments, but it was a long time before it was picked up in Middle Eastern religions as a primary objective.

Once it was, however, for more than two thousand years, the "Golden Rule", as it became known, remained the key guiding principle for most people on the planet. It has only been since the rise of individualism and the moral-less market place in the last half of the 20th Century that some think its influence on humankind has started to wane.

The first group of people to set out clear goals for themselves, that is, who identified desirable social improvements for everyone to strive for, rather than just set out a list of rules for people to abide by, appeared around the same time as Confucius, but in India. Around 500 BC both Buddhism and Modern Hinduism emerged and embraced the "six perfections" or goals of humanity; namely generosity, morality, tolerance, diligence, contemplation and wisdom.

As for the development of governments, up until this time, public decision-making was carried out almost entirely through monarchies, kingdoms, army commanders and other forms of one-man bands. However, around the same time that Confucius and Siddhartha Gautama were introducing their ideas to Asia and India, the Athenians were experimenting with democratic decision-making.

The Greeks were the first to formally give everyone, at least all free male citizens of Athens over the age of 30, the right to participate in public decision-making. There were no representatives involved. Decisions were made literally by the majority vote of the five thousand or more citizens who turned up at one of Athens' scheduled public meetings.

The reality was that less than 5% of the 200,000 people living in the city at the time actually participated in the process because most residents were slaves, women or children who didn't count. Still, the Athenian experiment lasted nearly 200 years. It showed that at least under some circumstances, majority vote decision-making could work as a way to make public decisions among large groups of people.

Over the next 1000 years two more major new religions, Christianity and Islam, embraced the Ten Commandments of Moses and the Golden Rule, but only Islam encouraged governmental reform to achieve a moral society.

It was not until the early thirteenth century when Britain's early drafts of the Magna Carta introduced the idea that even kings were not above the law, that Christian public decision-making caught up with Islamic efforts to coordinate government and social reform.

However, their similarity did not last long. While Islamic governments continued to integrate their decision-making with the morals of their religion, Christian governments then slowly and purposefully began to separate themselves from religion.

The separation of church from state was seen by some as a retrograde step for humanity and the end of morals in Western government decision-making, but it did allow Western governments the freedom to re-investigate the value of more democratic forms of public decision-making.

§

Probably the most dramatic moment in this search came in 1776, when America's Declaration of Independence proclaimed that all men were created equal and had the right to "Life, liberty and the pursuit of happiness".

Britain and a number of other countries had been

gradually working toward similar public goals for several centuries before this (particularly after John Locke's writings in the late 1600s) but the American Declaration of Independence suddenly grabbed the attention of the world, and since then, almost all new governments have used similar reasoning to justify their own existence.

Strangely, America's groundbreaking Constitution, written only four years after the American Revolution was won, actually makes no mention of the human rights that the Declaration of Independence championed and the war against Britain was supposed to secure.

Most of the language in the American Constitution is spent discussing how taxes and armies should be raised and how the election of the President and congressional representatives should take place.

Thankfully, the Bill of Rights, tacked onto the American Constitution as an after thought at the insistence of several States who would not sign the Constitution without it, mentions the right to life, liberty and property, but to this day there is still no mention of the right to the pursuit of happiness in the primary laws of the USA. The rights that were introduced as early amendments to the American Constitution included:

1. Freedom of speech,

2. Freedom of the press,

3. Freedom to peacefully assemble,

4. Freedom of religion,

5. Freedom to petition the government,

6. Freedom to bear arms,

7. Freedom from unreasonable search and seizure,

8. Due process of law including assistance of legal council,

9. Trial by jury (if the crime involves more than $20),

10 No excessive bail, fines, cruel or unusual punishment.

Just a few years after the American Revolution, the French led their own revolution with a rallying cry that sounded similar to America's. Their slogan was "Liberty, Equality, Fraternity".

However, it turned out to be fundamentally different. When the French motto was put into their own Declaration of Rights, it included the idea that there were social values worth protecting not just individual rights. In addition to the ten rights of Individuals included in the American version, the French Declaration of Rights included several provisions about equality and social justice not included in America's, such as:

1. All men are equal under law,

2. The aim of a community is the wellbeing of its people,

3. The role of Government is to guarantee public enjoyment of their rights,

4. Communities should support their unfortunate citizens, either by providing work or, for those unable to work, by other means,

5. Communities should provide education for all in order to advance public reason.

Many decades later, following the American Civil War, another amendment to the US Constitution was added to pick up the French "equal under law" right originally espoused in the American Declaration of Independence but left out of the American constitution so that slavery could remain legal.

For a decade in the early 20th Century, there was also an amendment to prohibit the consumption of alcohol in the USA, a prohibition that has existed in most Islamic countries for the last 1400 years. Under market place decision-making, however, the hard won social benefits of this amendment were difficult to quantify monetarily and the cost of its enforcement was soon easy to see, so it was quickly removed.

In the early 1940s, America's 32nd President, Franklin D Roosevelt, suggested the rights included in the American

Constitution should be extended to include a person's right to the pursuit of happiness. He wanted to add two new "social freedoms" to the US Constitution:

1. Freedom from want,
2. Freedom from fear.

As a late addition to his "New Deal" philosophy guiding the US through the Great Depression of the 1930s, he believed Americans should have the right to earn a reasonable living, and be able to do so without fear of war or other harassments.

§

Unfortunately, he did not manage to get his additional "freedoms" included in the Constitution during his lifetime, but three years after his death his ideas found their way into the United Nations Universal Declaration of Human Rights through the ongoing efforts of his wife, Eleanor Roosevelt. That document, adopted by most of the world since 1948, lists the following as basic human rights (paraphrased):

1. Everyone has the right to life, liberty and personal security,

2. Everyone is born free and equal,

3. No one's rights and freedoms are limited by race, color, sex, language, religion, opinion, origin, property, birth or other status,

4. Everyone has the right to freedom of movement and residence,

5. Everyone has the right to own property alone or collectively,

6. Everyone has the right to freedom of thought, conscience and religion,

7. Everyone has the right to freedom of opinion and expression,

8. Everyone has the right to peacefully assemble and associate with others,

9. Everyone has the right to free education, at least in the elementary stages,

10. Education shall promote understanding, tolerance and friendship among all,

11. Everyone has the right to participate freely in the cultural, arts and scientific life of the community,

12. Everyone has the right to take part in the government of their country, directly or through freely chosen representatives,

13. No one shall be arbitrarily deprived of his nationality nor denied the right to change his nationality,

14. No one shall be subjected to arbitrary interference with his privacy, family, home or correspondence,

15. No one shall be subjected to arbitrary arrest, detention or exile,

16. No one shall be subjected to torture or cruel treatment,

17. Everyone is presumed innocent until proved guilty under law by public trial,

18. Everyone has the right to work, freely chosen, under just and favorable conditions,

19. Everyone has the right to equal pay for equal work,

20. Everyone has the right to rest and leisure,

21. Everyone has the right to marry and have a family,

22. The family is the natural and fundamental unit of society and is entitled to protection by the State,

23. Motherhood and childhood are entitled to special care and assistance,

24. Everyone has the right of equal access to public services in their country,

25. Everyone is entitled to social and international order,

26. Everyone has the right to a standard of living adequate for the health and well-being of himself and of his family,

including adequate food, clothing, housing, medical care and necessary social services,

27. Everyone has the right to security in the event of unemployment, sickness, disability, widowhood, old age or other circumstances beyond his control,

28. Everyone has duties to the community including recognizing the rights and freedoms of others and of meeting the just requirements of morality, public order and the general welfare in a democratic society.

This list has been clarified and elaborated upon by a variety of later United Nations documents, the European Convention on Human Rights, The Universal Islamic Declaration of Human Rights and more recent Bills of Rights that a number of countries have passed into law to enact the UN Declaration. In India they are incorporated directly within its Constitution.

Unfortunately, not all countries have fully adopted these rights yet. The US Representative to the UN, for instance, voted to support the declaration when the UN adopted it. However, the US has never amended its Constitution to take them into account; so technically, it has no legal standing in US courts.

Other countries, like New Zealand, Canada and Great Britain, have adopted the provisions, but only as standard legislation. This means that the provisions can be called upon in a court of law. However, if they were ever seriously tested, they could be easily modified or removed by the government of the day.

Critics of the UN Declaration include some Muslim countries that do not agree that women should have the same rights as men. Others wish it had prohibited the death penalty and included the right to abstain from killing (pacifism).

Nevertheless, by the general support they now receive from most nations around the world, they suggest that the planet is starting to think about the wider issues of social justice and the public's right to the pursuit of happiness.

What is particularly interesting in the Universal

Declaration of Human Rights is the recognition in the last article (actually part 2 of Article 29 of the Declaration) that people not only have rights but have obligations as well. This article states that all people . . . *have an obligation to protect other people's rights and to contribute to the morality, public order and the general welfare of society.* [my emphasis]

It is one of the first times that an individual's obligation to recognize both the rights of others and the collective interests of communities, is succinctly stated outside religious texts like the Bible and Quran.

§

It is not surprising that the natural and physical environment is not discussed in America's Constitution since two hundred years ago there was little worry that the environment was a finite entity. Even when the United Nations was set up 77 years ago, the planet's finite characteristics were not obvious to everyone.

Some have been concerned about the limited resources of the planet for a while though. Planning pioneers, Patrick Geddes and Ebenezer Howard were both conscious of it more than 100 years ago. Today, thankfully, it is not just planners, but most human beings, who are aware of just how finite the resources of our planet are.

In today's world, the environment cannot afford to be left out of the goals for humanity and the rights and responsibilities that people must live by. Without a secure and stable natural and physical environment, human rights and the rights of communities will remain permanently vulnerable to those able to exploit them.

Today, many countries around the world have written into law the rights and responsibilities of people to protect and sustain the environment.

New Zealand was among the first to put the principle of environmental sustainability at the top of virtually all government decision-making. Their Resource Management Act originally adopted in 1991 stated as its primary purpose:

Managing the use, development and protection of natural and physical resources in a way, or at a rate which enables people and communities to provide for their social, economic, and cultural well-being and for their health and safety while-

(a) Sustaining the potential of natural and physical resources (excluding minerals) to meet the reasonably foreseeable needs of future generations; and

(b) Safeguarding the life-supporting capacity of air, water, soil, and ecosystem; and

(c) Avoiding, remedying or mitigating any adverse effects of activities on the environment.

§

It may help knowing that the planet seems to be working out a basic, consistent set of goals for the future of humanity, but it will probably take a lot more time and the input of many more people before they are firmly entrenched. However, at this point, there appears to be twelve of them:

1. Life
2. Liberty (Freedom)
3. Health
4. Happiness
5. Love (Tolerance)
6. Community (Friendship)
7. Purpose (Work)
8. Wisdom (Morality)
9. Justice (Honesty)
10. Security (Trust)
11. Peace
12. Environmental Sustainability

Chapter 10:

The Complexity of our Current Mess:

suggests that while the United Nations and other governments have brief lists of human rights for us all to live by, these lists are not nearly detailed enough to describe how humanity on this planet might get out of the deep mess it's in.

It is not that hard to pick out some of the bigger problems facing this planet today. To name just three:

> 1.   Our planet is overpopulated and the limited natural resources that support us are all rapidly dwindling.
> 2.   Individual access to water, food, shelter, energy, education, medical facilities, natural resources, justice and power around the planet is very inequitable, and this incites anger, violence and war between us.
> 3.   Social Darwinists suggest that our future, like our past, will be dictated by our innate cunning and greed, and there is little evidence to suggest they might be wrong.

I know, however, some people will not agree that even these three things are problems for the planet, or if they are, that anything collectively needs to be done about them.

Persuasive experts with vested commercial interests or strong religious beliefs today have little difficulty spreading untruths, just like the tobacco and oil companies did for years. What makes it particularly difficult for anyone hearing such experts is that often there is some real truth mixed in with the lies being told told to make it almost impossible to separate out what is fact from what is not.

For instance, many people now believe that man-made pollution is causing global warming and sea levels to rise, but some say this might actually be a good thing. They point out as an example of beneficial pollution, that for thousands of years local villagers living in the rugged highlands of Ethiopia have polluted the Nile River by their farming techniques.

Although this unique mountainous part of the African continent remains green most of the year and provides over 80% of the water in the lower Nile River, droughts do occur there. So local planting in Ethiopia has always been timed for the local equivalent of the Asian monsoon season.

Each year for thousands of years, while Ethiopian crops grew in the rain, the newly disturbed earth there was washed down into local streams and rivers and ultimately into the Nile, where it was eventually deposited in the floodplains of Egypt. At least it was until 1902 when the first Aswan Dam was built.

What then complicates the truth is that even expert historians will tell you that the ancient annual silt deposits along the Lower Nile Valley were at least partly responsible for the beginning of the Egyptian civilization and, in effect, the beginning of our own.

That is, what some would call the man-made pollution from Ethiopia has a lot to do with why some of us live in luxury today, why we can read and write, build cities, send ourselves to the moon and talk face to face with anyone on the planet by simply staring into a tiny computer.

The growing overpopulation predicament is another side of the same problem. Some estimates suggest that our planet can sustain at best only 1% of the people now on it if everyone had all the trappings of civilization that exist today, but still had to survive on its currently known resources.

There is both envy and fear among some Westerners toward how China tried to solve the problem. The Government there simply told everyone that no couple could have more than one child. During the decades that this instruction was enforced, local practices were not quite as absolute as the policy sounded, but still, it was a drastic measure to take.

China's Government isn't democratic but is not government enforced birth control an obvious solution to many of the Planet's problems? Is not China the ugly beast to some in the West precisely because it can fix some very serious problems that the rest of us now cannot, other than through the blunt instruments of our military and the market place?

§

So who, now, is responsible for deciding our future? Who, now, is responsible for determining what is truth and what is not? Should our future just be the consequence of ignorance or indecision? Should such decisions be left to God? Must rising sea levels or a nuclear holocaust be the unavoidable consequence of our inability to choose a better future for ourselves, or because of a belief or an uncorroborated assumption that we cannot change it, even if we wanted to?

Such complex questions and their possible implications are almost limitless, which is why the development of a new approach to democratic decision-making, one that forces decision-makers to consider consciously and rigorously the impact of their decisions on all things; on all types of change, on all goals of humanity, seems so important.

What is at stake here is not just our own personal health and wealth, but the very survival of our planet and the unique, global gift of human life that populates it. It is not just our physical surroundings and the tools we've learned to make for ourselves on the edge of the abyss now. It is the collective love, trust, and social justice that we human beings have managed to build among ourselves over the last few millennia despite our innate ability as individuals to be violent, ruthless, selfish and greedy, which is at stake here.

§

What follows next in the full edition of "Power Chaos or Consensus?", but not in this one because of the length and complexity of the subject, is an attempt to describe more than 50 of the most significant problems that I think humanity faces today. To help organize the discussion, each identified problem has been placed within one of the previously discussed systems of change; i.e. Personal, Economic, Equity, Community, and

Environmental change. Where relevant, I also described something I have experienced in my own life, to give some context.

My hope is that some people will be encouraged by the questions I've raised to find their own, better, more globally relevant solutions. It is why I have set up the website: www.consocracy.com and am looking for people willing to help arrange the questions that face us all into a form something like Wikipedia so that there can be wide public involvement in the development of global solutions.

§

Fortunately, for those who may be nervous about some of the solutions suggested, none of the ideas are set in stone. As will become clearer toward the end of this book, even if the suggested solutions are eventually adopted by a group of people, they can all be changed or entirely deleted by those affected by them, if they so wish.

For some of the suggested solutions, however, the ease with which they can be changed or deleted could be critical to successful consensus decision-making, so suggested solutions are identified in the next five chapters as either "Fundamental Solutions", "Recommended Solutions" or "Possible Solutions".

"Fundamental Solutions" are those that at this point seem essential to the successful operation of a consensus-based government and need to apply to everyone to allow it to work. Fundamental Solutions may be changed as experience proves or disproves their importance, but at least initially, they can only be changed by the consensus of the most senior or top most level of decision-makers in a structured consensus based government.

"Recommended Solutions" are those that would encourage peaceful co-existence between people, help achieve social justice or promote environmental sustainability. None are fundamental to the operation of a consensus-based government, but they might significantly improve it. They often include the verb "should" suggesting rather than dictating a right or responsibility. They can be removed by the consensus of any group of decision-makers at any time.

Initially, however they are included as part of the list of "Human Rights and Responsibilities" when making decisions.

All other solutions are "Possible Solutions" which at least initially have no status. Like Recommended Solutions, I believe they would encourage the peaceful co-existence of people, but because of existing religious or cultural differences on this planet, they may not be suitable for all groups of people, at least initially. They are set down more as questions that I believe every group will eventually need to debate and reach some form of mutual agreement on, although this is not essential to start with.

§

All of the global problems and possible solutions that are discussed in much more detail in the original "Power, Chaos or Consensus?" book but not in this one, are included because I believe a comprehensive discussion of the many major, multifaceted, and interconnected problems that we all face on this planet has to start somewhere. Getting into such detail, I think, is vital if we ever hope to find a way to live together in peace.

At this point, however, I cannot emphasize too much that it is the suggested "structured consensus decision-making" process that is of primary importance in this book, not any particular solution to one or more of the problems we face. Nevertheless, just using the decision-making ideas described so far will not fix the problems facing humanity unless we each, individually and collectively, also accept what these problems are and how to fix them.

As discussed in Chapter 9, the United Nations' Universal Declaration of Human Rights, now adopted by most countries around the world, contains a good list of basic human rights that we need to consider when making public decisions, but unfortunately, this "Universal Declaration of Human Rights" identifies few of the human "responsibilities" we also need to accept to ensure a peaceful future for ourselves.

There is a subtle but significant difference between "rights" and "responsibilities". Human "Rights" are things we are allowed to do to protect our own interests. Human

"Responsibilities" are things we must do to protect the interests of others.

Only the UN Declaration's last article, Part B of Article 29, suggests there are more than just human rights to consider. It says:

> "All people have an obligation [or responsibility] to contribute to the morality, public order and general welfare of society".

While a good start, this Article alone isn't sufficiently detailed to describe how we're going to fix the deep mess we're in. A much more exhaustive list of both human rights & human responsibilities needs to be added to the Goals of the consensus based government that has been described so far in this book.

Consideration of such details would allow all those who would like to participate in their own governance to do so following, as far as practicable, a single consistent, though amendable, locally and globally relevant set of guidelines.

§

So that is what Chapters 11-15 of the original "Power, Chaos or Consensus?" book (but not in this one) are really all about. They are about the identification of a comprehensive set of "rights and responsibilities" to guide all public decision-making. They do this by first identifying as many major problems facing the planet as possible and then suggesting solutions to resolve each one of them. Every solution is then simply expressed as a "right and responsibility".

The switch from "solution" to "right and responsibility" may sound problematic but it isn't. It is like saying "A solution to achieve peace is for everyone to stop killing others" and then saying "To achieve peace it is everyone's responsibility to stop killing others". The meanings of the two sentences are virtually identical, despite the word "solution" being replaced by the word "responsibility".

Expressing solutions to problems as "rights and responsibilities" allows each of us to take them into account when trying to achieve global peace, social justice, economic stability and environmental sustainability. When combined with the Goals and "Structured Consensus Decision-Making" process discussed earlier in this book, and the Principles and Structural Details discussed in Chapter 16 such solutions, or "Rights and Responsibilities", describe how each one of us, singly and together, might peacefully fix our planet.

Chapter 11: (Not included)

Personal Problems: *discusses sixteen problems involving personal matters that governments often try to control without any detailed understanding of their impact on specific individuals, including Fertility, Euthanasia, Elderly Care, Sensory Perception, Pleasure Drugs, Prostitution, Marriage, Discrimination, Mental, Physical and Social Disabilities, Violence and Abuse, Obesity, Privacy, Private Property, Carrying Arms, and Access to Food, Water and Shelter.*

Chapter 12: (Not included)

Economic Problems: *explores ten interconnected global economic problems that are contributing to the serious inequities now facing humanity, including how we now manage The Market Place, Work, Job Sharing, Corporations, Cooperatives, Currency, Interest, Tax Avoidance and Money Laundering, Limited Liability and Bankruptcy*

Chapter 13: (Not included)

Equity Problems: *Investigates twelve problems interfering with the development of peace on this planet including our forms of Government, Red Tape, Planning, Taking, Taxes, Language, Censorship, Armed Forces, Pacifism, Lawyers vs. Experts, Punishment and Justice.*

Chapter 14: (Not included)

Community Problems: *examines six basic global problems that can unintentionally but seriously affect social harmony, including the Media (social media and biased or fake news), Public Health Care, Public Education, Religious Persecution, Cultural Preservation and Social Support Systems for the unemployed, elderly and infirm.*

Chapter 15: (Not included)

Environmental Problems: discusses twelve interrelated environmental problems that we need to address if humankind is to have a long term future on this planet, including Resource Sustainability, Climate Change, Natural Hazards, Movement, Transportation Networks, Nodal Growth, Effects Based Development, Rural Land Use, Land Banking, Energy Use, Pollution and Recycling, and Hazardous Substances

.

Chapter 16:

The Principles and Structures of a Consensus Based Democracy:

describes the 5 basic principles of a consensus based democratic government. It defines several key terms like "site" and "public path" and it sets out a self-checking, self correcting set of "Structural Details" to ensure good governance in addition to the standard executive, legislative and judicial functions found in our current democracies.

There are five basic principles that once underpinned most democracies. Abraham Lincoln talked about the first one; that democratic governments should be of the people, by the people and for the people. This principle would seem self-evident, but it clearly it isn't. Almost none of the democratic governments that exist today are either "of" or "by" the people. They are only "of" and "by" the majority of those being governed. Those in the minority have virtually no say at all over many major life choices.

A second basic principle was that most decisions of government had to be voluntarily delegated to a number of representatives to make decision-making among large groups possible. It assumed that there will be enough representatives involved to allow all voters to have at least some personal knowledge of at least one of them.

Unfortunately, however, the huge population growth on this planet from one billion to eight billion people in just the last two centuries has meant that it is now almost impossible for anyone in a modern democracy to personally know any representative. Almost all of them today are little more than caricatures created by professional public relations experts.

A third basic principle that underpinned most democracies was that every public decision needed to take into account its consequences on all aspects of society, the environment and the market place. To this end, democratic governments have always relied on the advice of experts to consider the wider implications of their political decisions before making them. Unfortunately, such advice was, and often still is, only partial and inconsistent. For example, no democratic government today has a consistent way to decide whether spending $50 million dollars buying one heavily armed military drone is more important than providing food, housing, health care and education from birth to adulthood for 100 potential terrorist children. The costs are about the same.

It is why this book has spent so much time trying to identify a clearer, much more robust way of seeing the "big picture" of every public decision.

A fourth basic principle that once underpinned most democracies was that the individual (and where relevant his or her family) was the fundamental building block of a society's governance, rather than a king, state, culture, religion or race.

Within reason, individuals were free to pursue their own happiness and expected their government to protect this right. This, in fact, was one of the primary reasons why American Colonialists revolted against the rule of Britain's King George III two hundred fifty years ago and why most governments since then have tried to follow suit. Unfortunately, we are told today by those we now entrust with our governance that there are just too many of us now on this planet to allow everyone to have such freedom.

The fifth and final principle that once underpinned early village level democratic decision-making was that public decisions were best made by the consensus of the people affected by them, so that no one was left out. However consensus decision-making has never worked well in large groups so our modern governments looking after huge populations have turned to majority vote decision-making, which works with any size group of people. The unfortunate consequence of this "simpler" system is that it turns all minority groups into permanent losers, as humanity is only now discovering

§

While all five principles behind democratic governance have developed serious flaws in their use today, I believe they are still vital to the successful functioning of any true democracy.

As suggested earlier, there are probably many ways they could be re-introduced into our current governments, but the following 42 "Structural Details" set out below, describe how with care, patience and persistence, they could be progressively re-introduced into the structure of any existing democratic institution.

I view these "Structural Details" as equivalent to the articles in a government's constitution, although they are much more easily amended and don't include the equally important "Rights and Responsibilities" discussed in the book "Power, Chaos or Consensus?" The Structural Details below form the logic behind the detailed "Rules" included in the Consocratic Plan itself. Exactly how these details might be introduced into an existing democracy is described in Chapter 19.

Structural Detail 1.) Probably the most important structural detail of a Consocratic Government is that every individual in it must have a globally unique identification number similar to a passport number, and this number must be associated with a globally unique definable, publicly recorded three dimensional space called a "site". (not just a Post Office box number.) For most people, the associated "site" would be where ever the individual lives, but it doesn't have to be. It is up to the individual to decide what "site" he or she is associated with, and may change his or her association to another publically recorded "site" if others already associated with that other "site" accept the new association.

Structural Detail 2.) A "site" includes any privately owned but publicly accessible area of at least 500 ft^3 (15 m^3) with the least dimension of 8 ft (2.4 metres) under the control of a single person, family, business or other entity as described in public records, such as on property or vehicle titles. For instance, a site in a residential area would usually include a house and all associated land, but it might be just a squatter's shack in a slum, a camper van legally parked and occupied on public land or an apartment within a building provided there is permanent (24/7) public access to that shack, van or apartment's entrance. A gated community locked overnight, an old folks home with units only accessible from inside through a lockable front door, an indoor shopping mall closed and locked at night, or an industrial complex that restricts access to staff or invited guests, on the other hand, would all be considered single sites.

Structural Detail 3.) In most of the world today, almost all "sites" are now clearly identified by legal surveys, recorded titles, rectified aerial photographs or some other form of public documentation. However where there is none and an individual wanting to be associated with a site can show there is no other claim or association with it, and he or she has a legitimate association with that site, this documentation could simply be lines or 3D shapes drawn on a paper or internet generated map, which are then recorded electronically on public records.

Structural Detail 4.) Individuals often associate with other individuals for extended periods, such as when they create and raise children, so for the purpose of running a Consocracy, the number of people that may be associated with a single site is not a public concern. Essentially each site, and all those individuals associated with it, are autonomous under a Consocratic form of government if no one enters or leaves the site, no rights of an individual within it are threatened and most importantly, nothing within a site has any effect on the environment (including people) outside it, unless all those affected outside of it agree to this.

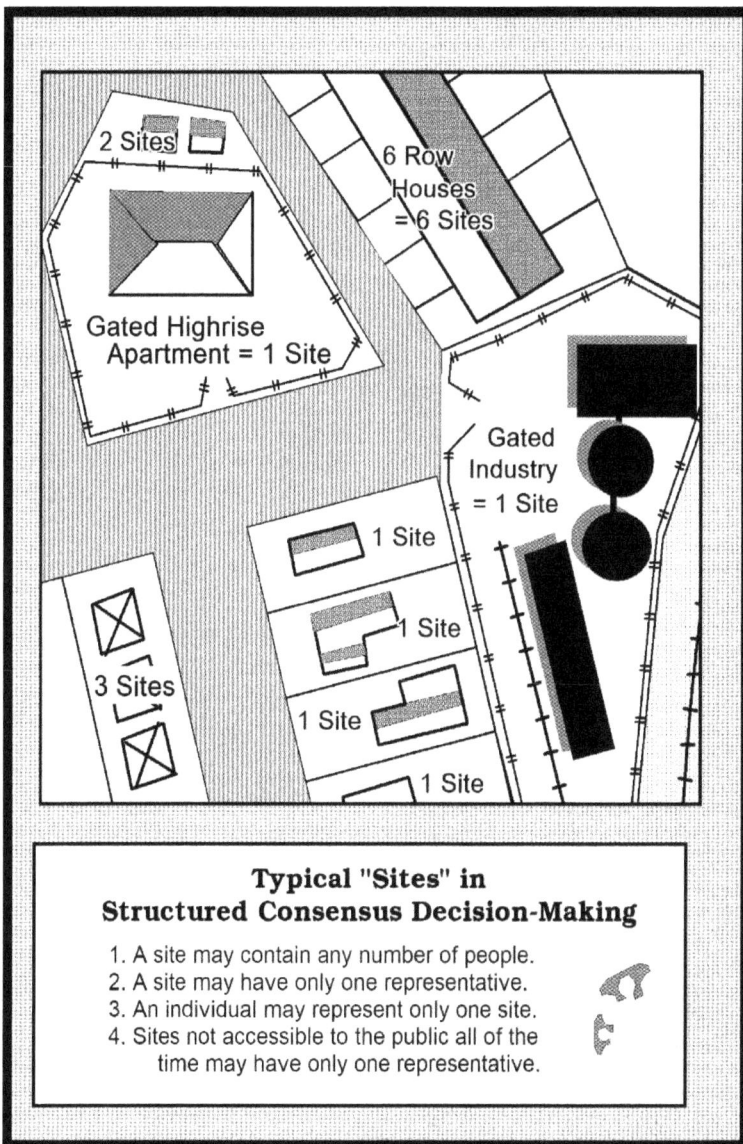

2 Sites

6 Row Houses = 6 Sites

Gated Highrise Apartment = 1 Site

Gated Industry = 1 Site

1 Site

1 Site

3 Sites

1 Site

1 Site

Typical "Sites" in Structured Consensus Decision-Making

1. A site may contain any number of people.
2. A site may have only one representative.
3. An individual may represent only one site.
4. Sites not accessible to the public all of the time may have only one representative.

117

Structural Detail 5.) Communally owned land and other very large single sites occupied by many people may be split into multiple sites if each of the new sites created is publicly accessible all of the time (24/7) and is recorded on public records. However, splitting up any large site into multiple smaller sites is not mandatory.

Structural Detail 6.) A business may be represented in a Consocracy if the site where it is located has an individual living within it willing to represent its interests, or if an individual living elsewhere chooses to associate him or herself with the site where the business is located and others already associated with that site (if any) accept the new association.

Structural Detail 7.) An Individual's association with a site determines where and how that individual or business may participate in a Consocratic Government.

Of particular importance:

   a.) An individual may not be associated with more than one site, and equally important,

   b.) A "site" may not have more than one representative on the lowest level of a Consocratic Government.

Structural Detail 8.) Just like existing "local", "regional" and "central" governments, a Consocratic government has multiple levels of representation. The ultimate number of levels in any Consocratic government will depend on the total number of represented sites involved and the total number of people being governed in any group. The table below sets out the minimum number of sites and minimum number of people represented in a group on any given level. Note that the number of levels suggested below to run the world is no more than the number of government levels that now exists in most parts of the world.

Minimum number of sites and people represented

Individual/Household (site)	1 site	(1 person)
Level 1 Group (Neighborhood)	10 sites	(10 people)
Level 2 Group (Village)	100 sites	(100 people)
Level 3 Group (Town)	1,000 sites	(1,000 people)
Level 4 Group (City)	10,000 sites	(10,000 people)
Level 5 Group (Region)	100,000 sites	(100,000 people)
Level 6 Group (State)	1,000,000 sites	(1,000,000 people)
Level 7 Group (Country)	10,000,000 sites	(10,000,000 people)
Level 8 Group (Continent)	100,000,000 sites	(100,000,000 people)
Level 9 Group (World)	1,000,000,000 sites	(1,000,000,000 peop)

Structural Detail 9.) All decisions made within an individual site may be reached by any method. For instance, for the selection of a site's representative, if only a single household occupies the site and it is a family dominated by a traditional patriarch, its representative on the first level of government might well be the father or grandfather. If the site is a publicly accessible (24/7) apartment of a woman living alone, she will be its representative. Where the site contains only a business, it is up to the business to find an individual willing to accept being associated with that site. If this association happens to be with the traditional patriarch described in the first example, then the site with the patriarch's household must be represented by someone other than the patriarch, such as his wife or adult child, as one individual (the patriarch in this case) cannot be associated with two different sites. There is no minimum age of a representative although other qualifications such as minimum education may be required. It is up to those associated with a site to decide how its representative in a Group on the first level of a Consocratic Government is chosen.

Structural Detail 10.) Between 6 and 42 site representatives on adjacent sites may come together to form a decision-making Group on the lowest level, that is, a Level 1 (Neighborhood) Group, and make consensus based

119

decisions on all matters that affect only the sites and the individuals they represent. There will be a natural tendency for Groups to be as large as possible initially, as the larger the Group the larger the area that a Group may control. However, it will become apparent to Group members that it is difficult to reach consensus in a large group. Smaller Groups work better.

Structural Detail 11.) A site representative's choice as to whether he or she joins an existing Group, creates a new one or switches from one to another may be based on common interests with other representatives, such as a common language, religion, culture or extended family, but there doesn't have to be any reason. A site representative may join any Group on the first (Neighborhood) level provided that:

    a.)   The representative's site is contiguous to, or directly across a public path or other public land from at least one other site represented by the Group being joined or created, and

    b.)   The Group being joined or created contains not less than 6 or more than 42 members. If a Group contains more than 42 members when joined by a new site representative, it must divide into at least two Groups, all with 6 members or more.

Structural Detail 12.) No site, activity or individual that any Level 1 (Neighborhood) Group represents may affect any site, activity or individual beyond their joint physical borders without the permission of all those affected beyond that Group (or their representatives). For first level government Groups, the matters that they can control are very local and initially will probably only involve issues between neighbors, like the location of a new building or a change of site use by a neighbor. In a fully developed Consocracy, however, level 1 (neighborhood) Groups will also be able to determine many other matters of local importance such as what social support services a sick, handicapped or elderly individual in their neighborhood might receive, or what would be suitable punishment and compensation for a neighbor's petty theft.

Structural Detail 13.) To decide upon matters affecting anything outside the jurisdiction of a Level 1 (Neighborhood) Group, the site representatives on the first level of government must select by consensus from among themselves a single individual to represent their interests in a decision-making Group on a second level of government, known as Level 2 (Village) Groups.

Structural Detail 14.) Like Level 1 Groups, the number of representatives in a second level (Village) Group must not be less than 6 or more than 42 individuals. Also like Level 1, the only two requirements are that the sites he or she represents must be contiguous to, or directly across a public path/public land from at least one other site represented by the decision-making Group being joined or created, and if the joined Group then contains more than 42 members it must split into at least 2 Groups each with no less than 6 members. This structure is repeated on every subsequent level of government created, forming the "structured consensus decision-making" discussed in chapter 7. It is repeated on all levels.

Structural Detail 15.) There is one significant difference between the first three levels of decision-making and those above the third level. Above level three, there is no requirement at the fourth (City) level that all representatives making up any Group of decision-makers must come from contiguous areas. They may come from anywhere. Until Consocratic theory is better understood, the practical limit of "anywhere", is any other city, state or country, but ultimately it could mean anywhere on the planet. Decisions made by every level of government only apply to those sites they represent, so while site contiguity is not mandatory above level three, there is strong motivation for all sites represented to still be contiguous with each other where there are no social, cultural or religious reasons not to be. On the other hand, the structure of a Consocracy would work even if every level of decision-making including levels 1, 2 and 3, involved sites that were not contiguous. The requirement that all sites on the first three levels must be contiguous is just to simplify implementation of the theory. It is entirely possible that in time, a Consocracy could evolve to be entirely site specific on every level.

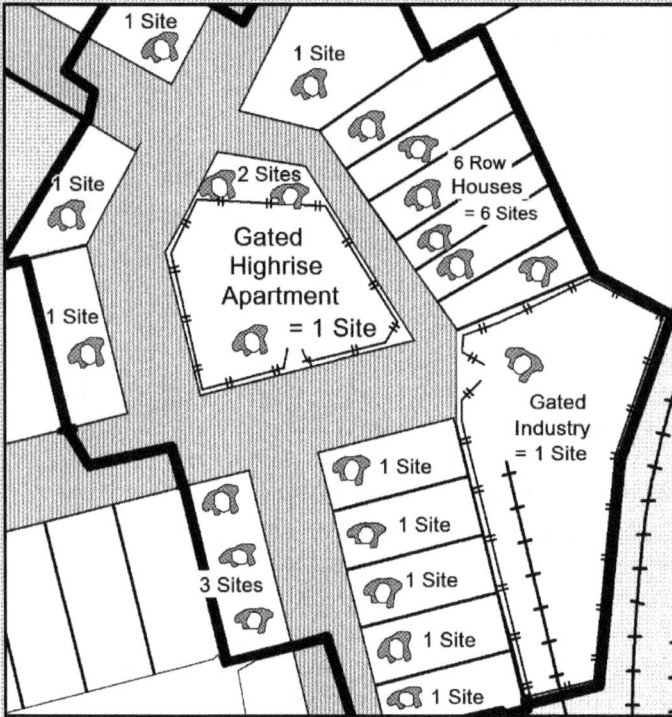

A Typical Level 1 "Neighborhood" Group in Structured Consensus Decision-Making

1. A Level 1 Neighborhood Group must contain between 6 and 42 representatives representing between 6 and 42 sites
2. Representatives from any adjacent site may join this group.
3. If a Neighborhood Group grows larger than 42 representatives it must split into two or more Groups on Level 1.

Structural Detail 16.) There is no obligation for any site to be represented by an associated person in a Consocratic government. Some sites might not have anyone interested in being associated with them or might contain only people who do not wish to participate in government.

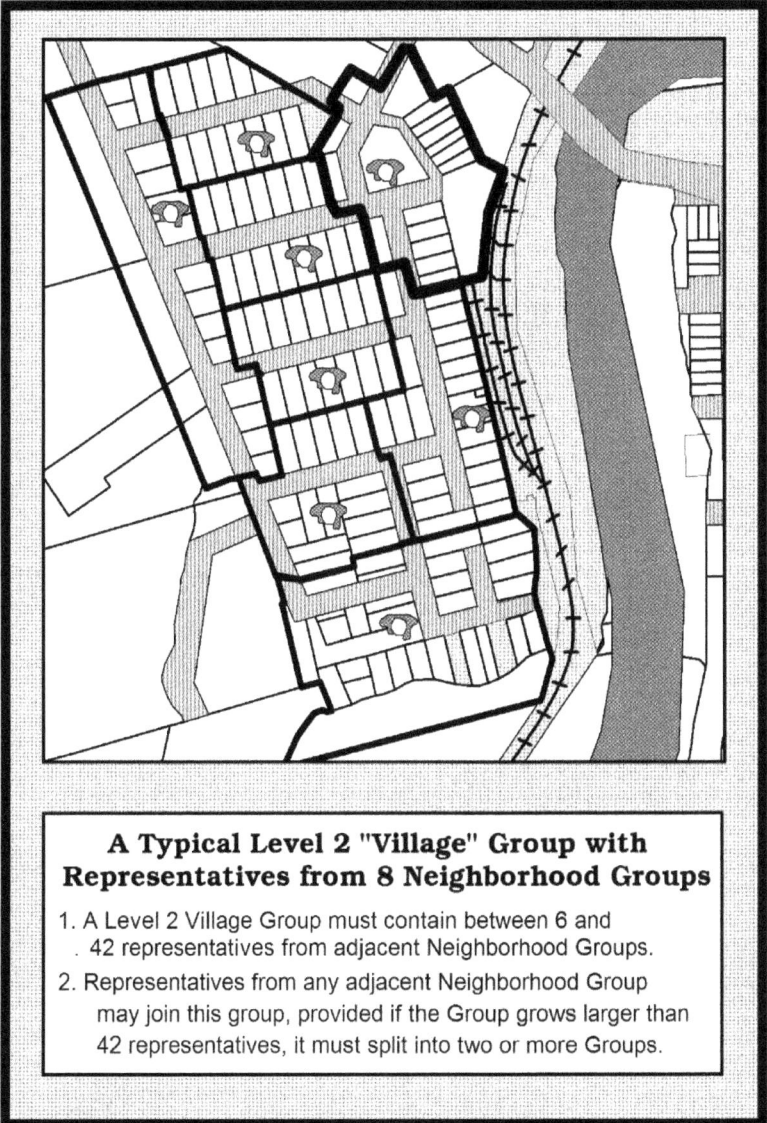

A Typical Level 2 "Village" Group with Representatives from 8 Neighborhood Groups

1. A Level 2 Village Group must contain between 6 and
 . 42 representatives from adjacent Neighborhood Groups.
2. Representatives from any adjacent Neighborhood Group
 may join this group, provided if the Group grows larger than
 42 representatives, it must split into two or more Groups.

Unless an individual associated with a site chooses to participate in a Consocratic Government, those sites and the individuals within them have no direct say in what happens if something or someone within their site affects something or someone outside that site.

A Typical Level 3 "Town" Group with Representatives from 10 Village Groups

1. A Level 3 Town Group must contain between 6 and
   . 42 representatives from adjacent Village Groups.
2. Representatives from any adjacent Village Group
   may join this group, provided if the Group grows larger than
   42 representatives, it must split into two or more Town Groups.

Structural Detail 17.) Sites that have no representative are still subject to all decisions and rules made on their behalf by representatives of the sites physically closest to them. If more than one site with a representative physically borders a site without a representative, then it is the government Group that shares the greatest length of border with the unrepresented site that assumes responsibility for managing its external effects.

Structural Detail 18.) Decisions that are made by an affected Group which are designed to stop, rectify, mitigate and/or recover from the effects of another site's activity may be enforced and the cost of compliance, as well as deterrent penalties, may be imposed on all those associated with the site creating the effects.

Structural Detail 19.) In addition to associating every individual with a site, another very important detail in the structure of a Consocracy is that every site must have direct access to a clearly defined, "Public Path", such as a public road, public alley, public hallway, or other means that allows an individual to move without impediment from one site to any other site at all times, and for every site to have access to available public utilities, services and facilities at all times.

Structural Detail 20.) Overseeing the installation, maintenance and management of public paths, utility corridors, public facilities and community services are important functions of a Consocratic government, just as they are with most existing governments. In a Consocracy their provision and maintenance is undertaken by the level of government that fully includes them, although on the lowest levels, some responsibilities may be delegated to a higher level of government to improve the efficiency of their provision. Local streets, for instance, might technically be able to be built and maintained by a group on level 1 or 2 (Neighborhood or Village), but to minimize equipment and maintenance costs it might make sense to delegate such work to a Level 3 (Town) Group or higher.

Structural Detail 21.) Public utilities, services and facilities include schools, medical facilities, parks and open space, recreational facilities, transportation hubs, paths and networks, power/energy supplies and networks, water supplies and networks, liquid and solid waste collection and treatment and other utilities, services and facilities accessible to more than a single site. They do not have to be publicly owned. However, all publicly used utilities, services and facilities, even those privately owned, may be controlled (regulated) by public government.

§

Structural Detail 22.) Every meeting of a governing Group must contain a minimum of six representatives, five of them individually and separately advocating for one of the 5 types of "systems" of change discussed earlier, that is; Personal, Economic, Equity, Community and Environmental systems of change. The sixth member provides the link to another group. Each of the five "system" advocates must have been assigned specific responsibility for one set of systems at an earlier group meeting, so that he or she understands and can advocate for that set of systems at any group meeting. If a group contains more than six members, responsibility for each of the five sets of systems must be shared as needed among the other available members in the group.

Structural Detail 23.) The required 6th member of every group is the group's "Representative" and has no specific "systems of change" responsibilities in the group that chooses him or her. The individual's role is to represent the collective interests of that group in a group on the next level of government. Once the 6th member of a group becomes a member of a second group, both groups are then automatically linked together. This link provides a channel for information to freely pass in either direction between the two groups. More importantly, with the use of consensus decision-making, the linked member is in a position to directly affect the content of the decisions reached by both groups.

Structural Detail 24.) Any group (on any level) which drops below 6 members must disband and may not participate in public decision-making, although the individual members of the disbanded group may then join any adjacent group(s) on the same level. If any group exceeds 42 members, some or all of them must be shuffled into smaller groups on the same level. If one or more new groups are created doing this, they must then each contain at least 6 members with its own representative on the next level.

Structural Detail 25.) An individual may be involved in only two groups, a lower group and an upper group. In the lower group the individual's only responsibility is to represent the interests of the lower group in the upper group. In the upper group that same individual must take on one of the leadership roles listed in Structural Detail 26 below. If the lower group's representative is chosen to be the upper group's representative in an even higher level group, then that representative's responsibilities and involvement in the lower group cease immediately. The only exception to the 2 group limit of an individual, is that he or she may voluntarily become the representative of a sub-group. (See also Structural Detail 29)

Structural Detail 26.) Every Group on every level must assign or renew annually eleven (11) leadership roles for its members, similar to ministerial or cabinet responsibilities in a 21st century democracy. In addition to the representatives' role set out in Structural Detail 23, these leadership roles must be selected by the consensus of the same group that selects the main representative, and if a role is vacated for any reason, it must be filled prior to any further decision made by that group. In addition to the main representative, the leadership roles include alternate representative, chairperson, publicist, environmentalist, economist, public employer, lobbyist, ombudsist, arbiter and chief officer.

    a) The Alternate Representative ensures continuity of representation by being able to temporarily fill-in for the main representative in his or her temporary absence, or permanently replace the representative immediately upon his or her resignation, death, or selection by the higher group to an even higher level of governance. The Alternate Representative may never be the same gender as the main representative.

b) The Chairperson is responsible for calling, coordinating, mediating and running group meetings.

c) The Publicist is responsible for providing group record keeping and group liaison with public media.

d) The Environmentalist is responsible for providing planning and resource management advice to the group, including on matters such as the physical infrastructure of education and healthcare facilities, public utilities and the public path network.

e) The Economist is responsible for providing taxation, finance, and business advice to the group.

f) The Public Employer is responsible for the operational management of education and healthcare facilities and the public path network, and has the authority to employ any one out of work in the public sector at a "living wage".

g) The Lobbyist is responsible for passing on information, views and opinions to the group from any individual, business or other interest outside the group.

h) The Ombudsist has the right to independently review, investigate and publicize his or her conclusions regarding any public decision made by any lower level group represented by someone in that Ombudsist's group. The Ombudsist alone may not force a lower level group to change its decision, but the full Ombudsist's group, by consensus, may require a lower level group's decision to be reconsidered by a higher level group if the effects of the lower level group's decision are likely to go beyond its jurisdiction.

i) The Arbiter is responsible for providing group liaison with the activities of the Court.

j) The Chief Officer is responsible for providing group liaison with emergency services and the activities of the police-peace force.

§

Structural Detail 27.) While a Consocratic Government would ideally start when representatives from adjacent individual sites voluntarily gather together in small "Neighborhood" sized groups, such groups could be set up by a higher level of government, like a state or country. If started this way, the initial geographical extent of each "Neighborhood" sized group, would be relatively easy to identify using census data and existing property ownership maps. Each group would still select its own representative and other leadership roles and other higher levels would be established independently by affected groups as previously described.

Structural Detail 28 The absolute maximum size of a group is 42 representatives. This is because every member of a group must be able to sit together in a single circle and be able to see and hear all other members of the group without the aid of electronic devices. This effectively limits the practical maximum size of any group to around 30 people, although there may be some circumstances where this limit may need to be exceeded with the consensus of that groups members, particularly on the first two levels of a Consocratic government. There are two exceptions to the prohibition on the use of electronic devices in groups. They are:

a) Any or all members of a group containing 36 members or less may use electronic hearing aids to discretely improve poor hearing or to allow access to translation services, and

b) All members in a group containing 36 members or less may use electronic screens with microphones and speakers to see and hear everyone in the group using programs like Zoom or Skype, provided that all members are shown together in real time, each person with a similar sized head facing forward.

§

Structural Detail 29.) Like politicians today, group representatives do not have to be experts in any of the five types of systems or in any other matter. They can rely on the support of Engineers, Planners, Accountants, Education and Health Professionals, Administrators and other non-elected advisors where needed. Using experienced and knowledgeable people will help representatives take into consideration Personal, Economic, Equity, Community and Environmental effects of change in every group decision. Such advisors may be selected by any method but may not participate directly in any group decision-making unless permitted by the group as the representative of an approved sub-group.

Structural Detail 30.) Sub-groups may be formed on any single level of a Consocracy with the consensus of the main group to add expert knowledge to the group's decision-making. The sub-group must either be represented by the main group member in the leadership role that is most closely associated with that sub-group, or by the consensus of the group, filled by someone selected by the consensus of the sub-group's members. Sub-groups must emulate, as far as practicable, the structure and consensus decision-making of a Consocracy, and the number of represented sub-groups on any level is at the discretion of the main group, provided the main group's overall size does not exceed 42 individuals.

Structural Detail 31.) To help reduce the opportunity for narcissistic, aggressive or otherwise socially handicapped individuals to participate in government, level 1 (neighborhood) and level 2 (village) representatives are voluntary positions, although individuals may be paid the "living wage" if otherwise unemployed. They would be supported where needed by the administrative staff of Group Level 3 (Town). In addition, the only way any individual would be able to participate in any group decision-making above Level 1 would be by being selected by consensus as a Level 1 group's representative on Level 2 and then being selected as a group's representative again at every level above this. This would help to ensure that there is rigorous and repeated assessment of every individual's performance and suitability to be a group's representative at every level of government.

Structural Detail 32.) To further reduce the opportunity for socially handicapped individuals to become representatives and also to ensure there is gender parity on all levels of decision making, the alternate representative in any group must always be a different gender from the representative of that group.

Structural Detail 33.) Above Level 2, all representatives and their advisors must be paid salaries at a level commensurate with their responsibilities to ensure that they have adequate time and commitment to make good public decisions. The scale, location and type of administrative and technical support to help representatives make good decisions is determined by the responsibilities of the group, the population served and the complexities of the problems faced.

Structural Detail 34.) Because there are multiple levels of responsibility in structured consensus decision-making, consideration of the effects on any given level need not be a complex process. It simply requires each representative in any group, with the support of any advisors they may rely on, to evaluate what the effects of a proposed change or existing unapproved change might be on the systems under his or her responsibility, and then point them out to the other decision-makers in their group before all representatives in that group collectively make up their minds what to do.

Structural Detail 35.) For representatives in Level 1 government groups, pointing out effects might simply involve describing what his or her initial "gut feelings" are about a proposed new house or shop in the neighborhood. While Level 1 and 2 representatives would have access to the resources available to Level 3 Groups, they would not need to be utilized. Because of the very limited effects of any decision made by the first two level groups, the consequences of getting it wrong are not likely to be very large what ever is decided.

Structural Detail 36.) If an activity has or might have an effect beyond the site on which it is located, such as a proposed noisy industrial use in a residential neighborhood, it would not be a Level 1 neighborhood group that decides whether the activity is permitted. It would be a decision of one of the higher levels of government whose members represent all those who might be affected by the noise, traffic, pollution and other possible effects of the proposed activity. Bearing in mind that final decisions must be made by consensus, if anyone in a group raises a problem that he or she feels needs to be resolved, no change can take place and no existing activity producing the effect may continue until a solution is found that no one in the highest level group affected, opposes.

Structural Detail 37.) Most activities have effects that are easily identifiable and clearly relate to particular geographic areas. Those activities whose effects are not easy to define or physically locate, or whose effects can change with new technology, need not be a problem, however. The responsibilities of each level of government are not fixed in any way and can be temporarily or permanently handed on, without question, to the next higher level group through its representative link. Flexibility is further assisted by the fact that most decisions only need to be made once. With consensus decision-making, the endless delays caused by aggrieved groups appealing decisions to ever-higher authorities is unlikely to ever become a major concern.

Structural Detail 38.) The right of appeal for all groups does exist in a Consocracy, and it is very straight forward. It simply involves a representative continuing to oppose the position taken by the other members of a group. If, after full discussion (including where possible use of the Delphi

Technique, delegated negotiation, or more complex computer based problem-solving techniques (such as Weaver, Loomio or Value Knowledge Management) consensus cannot be reached among all members of a particular group, responsibility for the decision simply moves to the next higher level of government through that group's representative, accompanied by detailed written arguments from all group members with an interest in the decision. See also the Ombudsist role in reviewing poor decisions set out in Structural Detail 28.

Structural Detail 39.) An important qualification of structured consensus decision-making is that just because one group decides to allow an activity in one area it does not mean another group would have to allow the same thing in another similar area. There is nothing to stop a group from using past decisions to help it make its own decision-making easier, but in recognition of the uniqueness of every individual, locality, culture, time and place, there is no legal "precedence" set by any decision of any group.

§

Structural Detail 40.) To ensure continuity of government over time and to minimize disruption to decision-making, a new representative may not become a formal member of a governing group immediately. A representative must attend at least 6 meetings of the group being joined and fully respond to its member's questions before he or she may participate in formal consensus decision-making in that group, unless this apprenticeship is waived by the consensus of the other members of that group.

Structural Detail 41.) There is no maximum length of a representative's term of office and the term may continue for as long as the group he or she represents chooses by the annual consensus of the other members of the group, and with the representative's agreement.

Structural Detail 42.) The minimum term length of a group representative is one year to ensure some continuity in a group, although if the remainder of the group that selects the representative determines there has been intentional wrongdoing by that representative, the representative may be removed by the others immediately. Wrongdoing includes deliberately not upholding any Goal, Principle, Right, Responsibility or Rule of the Consocratic Plan.

§

The diagram on the following page is a snapshot of the structure of a Consocracy showing 4 levels of decision-making groups (Neighborhood, Village, Town and City) and how they relate to each other. Every black circle is a decision-making group of representatives. The size of the circle identifies the number of sites (and number of people) it represents; the larger the circle, the more sites (and people) represented.

Each black circle or decision-making group is set out and operated in the same way as every other black circle or group. The large black circle in the middle of the diagram is simply a detailed look at one of the decision-making groups on level 3. All groups on all levels actually look and operate like this.

As shown in the large detailed black circle in the middle, every circle or group is split into 6 sections. Five of the sections are labeled "Personal", "Economic", "Equity", "Community" and "Environmental" (PEECE) for the 5 types of systems of change each group decision must consider, and each of these sections contains two shaded and labeled ovals. One of the 6 sections of each black circle or group is only labeled "Representative".

This person provides the "link" between that group and a group on the next level of government, but takes no direct responsibly for any of the 5 types of systems of change on the lower level. The thin grey arrows represent the link that the same individual provides between the two groups on different levels.

In addition to the group's representative, every other member in a group must take on one of the ministerial or cabinet roles, which are the variously shaded ovals within the black circles. For groups with less than 11 members some of these roles must be doubled up. For instance the member responsible for economic systems in a group with less than 11 members may have to take on both the Economist and the Lobbyist roles

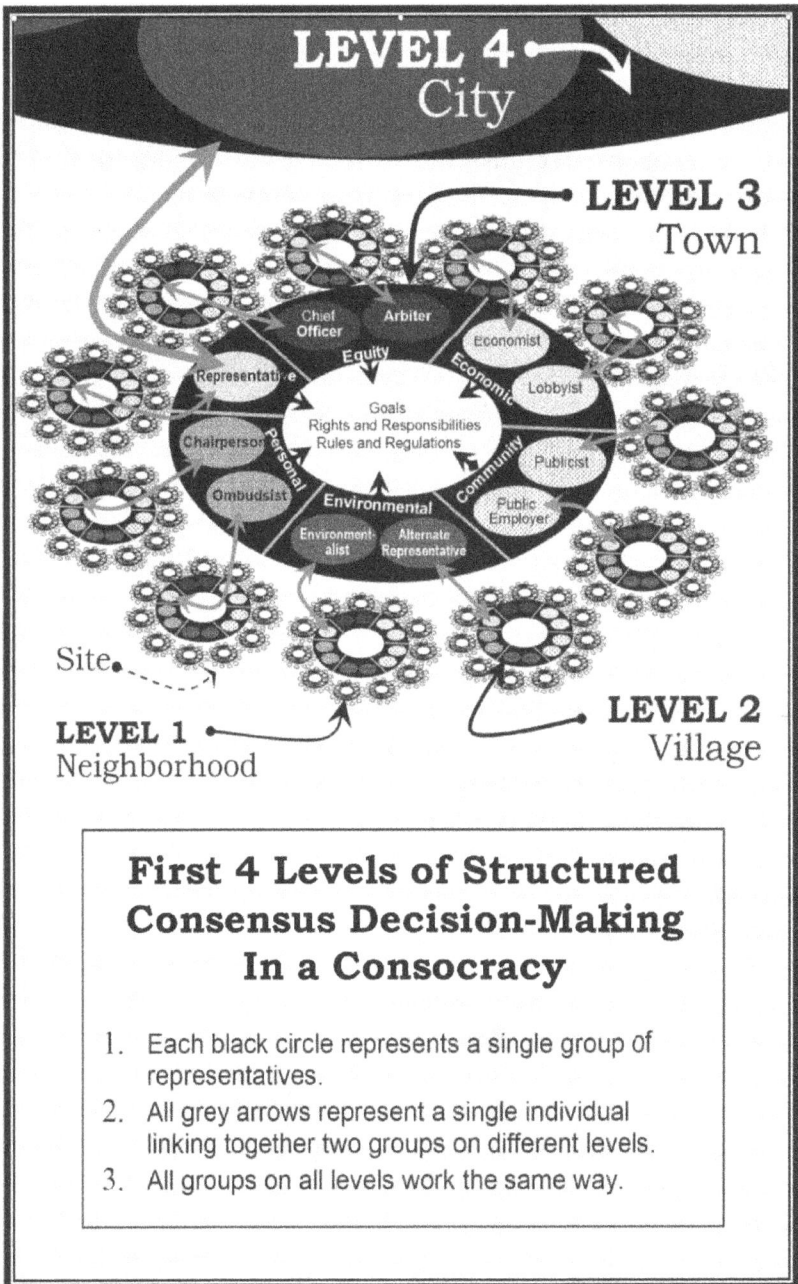

LEVEL 4 City

LEVEL 3 Town

LEVEL 2 Village

LEVEL 1 Neighborhood

Site

First 4 Levels of Structured Consensus Decision-Making In a Consocracy

1. Each black circle represents a single group of representatives.
2. All grey arrows represent a single individual linking together two groups on different levels.
3. All groups on all levels work the same way.

135

For groups larger than 11 members, cabinet or ministerial roles should be held jointly.

What is most important is that at least one group member responsible for each of the 5 types of systems of change, as well as the representative linked to the upper level group must all be present and involved in every decision made by that group. For this reason all groups must contain a minimum of 6 representatives, shown by the 6 short arrows into the centre of the black circle which link the decisions of every member to the goals, principles, rights, responsibilities, rules and regulations applicable to that group. Preferably, groups should not contain more than 30 members so that all representatives may easily talk together face to face with each other, although up to 42 members is permissible with the consensus of all group members.

Chapter 17:

The Financial Implications:
discusses several possible modifications to institutional finance that could be made to a new government which uses consensus decision-making to improve democratic outcomes. These include eliminating easily evaded income and business taxes and replacing them with a fixed "Resource Use Tax" and a "Goods and Services Tax", introducing the "Living Wage" in exchange for guaranteed, mutually agreed work in the public sector and providing social, medical and old age support services to all, primarily through a two tiered monetary system.

Technically, when a Consocracy is fully functioning, virtually all our existing public health systems, education systems, social security systems and other public services and facilities now in operation around the world could continue without increasing any taxes anywhere.

In fact, the best public systems and services now in existence could be expanded to cover the entire planet because there would no longer be any need to spend considerable sums of public money maintaining global armies to keep the peace. There would still need to be some police force in operation, but as the UN chart in Chapter 3 graphically pointed out, today we spend twice as much money on our military as we would need to spend to fix all the global problems we now face on this planet.

Such improvements would also be possible because much of the work now done today by minor government red tape makers, particularly those working on levels 1 & 2, would be done by volunteers or staff working at a relatively low "living wage".

Most importantly, however, under a Consocratic government, entirely new public revenue generating systems could be developed to replace the seriously outdated public revenue generating methods we now use today. Almost all of those now in use were originally introduced to pay for fixing a particular problem faced at a particular point in time.

Income and business taxes, for instance were first introduced more than two centuries ago to pay for war. As time progressed, however, both war finance tools have been expanded to build roads, pay for social services, protect the environment and support other public institutions. While their original use was intended to be short term, most of the programs now financed by them are designed to meet very different long term public needs.

The problem with this is that income and business taxes, from their very beginning, have always been notoriously difficult to collect equitably. The rich can afford to pay for experts to minimize or avoid paying them altogether, while the poor cannot afford such advice and invariably end up paying a disproportionately large amount to the government to keep public services (and wars) running.

Although it admittedly borders on being utopian, it is technically possible to remove taxes on individual earnings and business profits and replace them with something much more targeted to their purpose. For instance, a Resource Use Tax (RUT) on the use or exchange of all resources such as land and minerals, and a "value added" Goods and Services Tax (GST) on the purchase or exchange of virtually everything else, would produce very different results and be a great deal fairer way to pay for most public expenses. While this may sound unfair to the poor because they spend a much larger percentage of their income on necessities, there are multiple ways to offset such such effects on the poor.

If a GST value added tax is introduced, I think there probably should be only one GST tax rate collected on absolutely all goods and services. This has worked very well over the last 25 years in New Zealand. But "everything" should include the sales of all stocks, bonds, shares, ownership rights, capital gains, intellectual property, inheritances, insurances and businesses, which tax lawyers can now easily hide in trusts, off shore accounts and other tax evasion schemes. The only GST free exception should be that

GST should not be required on the purchase of a family's primary residence, as this significant purchase can act as an insurance policy for its occupants in unexpectedly difficult times.

A resources use tax would include taxes on the use of, or impact on, all land, air and water, all endangered plants and animals, and all minerals, liquids and gasses. At the moment, most tax systems encourage their short term exploitation rather than their long term conservation.

When applied to a community successfully using a Consocratic form of government, these two taxes would be collected at every level of government, and redistributed by the highest level of government to each lower level of government in varying amounts proportionate to the services each level provides. For instance, those earning the "living wage" might be paid through the "Public Employer" on the 1st or 2nd Level of government, public high school teachers might be paid through the "Public Employer" on the 4th or 5th Level.

Both RUT and GST taxes would require creating a clear public record of who owns or is associated with every public and private site and resource. Keeping such a record is one of the key Structural Details of a consensus based government described in the previous chapter. All individuals must be associated with a site that is recorded on public records so identifying and recording resource or site ownership and use would just require adding another electronic layer to these records using a GIS program (Geographical Information System) like MapInfo, ESRI, ARC or Google Earth.

This information would ensure that an individual, corporation or government is able to be held responsible in perpetuity for all liabilities attached to a particular site.

§

The wide variety of financial systems in operation today supporting public utilities, facilities, services, roads, schools, medical facilities, old age pensions, unemployment benefits and government administration, make it difficult for decision makers to deal holistically with any of them. Although not a fundamental component of a consensus based government, I believe governments should provide and maintain for free (paid in full by public taxes) only their own administration costs and the cost of providing public paths/roads, public open space/art galleries/libraries, public protection services (police), public media services (including internet access), emergency health services, and basic public education services through age 17. All of these should be paid for using only RUT and GST taxes (or the second level receipt system earned through payment of GST on essential goods.

Some other public services such as basic health care other than emergency services, basic recreational facilities, and essential utilities would be subsidized to reduce and even out delivery costs to affordable levels for all through the use of RUT and GST taxes, but would still have an access fee to use them so that they are not exploited or abused.

Other than this, there would be no public welfare system; no unemployment benefits, no disability benefits, no solo parent benefits, no old age pensions, or other similar social giveaways except in extreme circumstances, such as when a person is severely mentally or physically disabled.

What I believe should be available to every one over the age of 17 is the guarantee of work, usually but not necessarily, in the public sector at a locally set "living wage" that ensures just and reasonable living conditions for all adults and their dependent families. It would include sufficient funds to cover the entry fees for health care and other subsidized public services.

Because the job recipient would be personally known to those in the Level 1 or 2 group setting up the job, even though the pay was fixed at a "living wage", the job itself could vary considerably in duration or difficulty and could be fine-tuned to the particular interests, skills, age, abilities and responsibilities of each person.

Within reason the choice of work would be up to the recipient of the "living wage" and could involve work that was not traditionally considered valuable, such as raising children, working for public charities, creating pubic art works and providing social company to the elderly or infirm.

§

Access to specialist education and training, specialist health care, use of major recreational or transportation facilities such as stadiums, trains, toll roads and utilities using natural gas, petrol and other non renewable resources would be paid by the user at full cost.

Everyone would pay for all or part of the cost to use a public utility, facility or service using a special second level monetary system which involved the issuance of detailed personalized GST receipts on the purchase of food and other "essential items" Thanks to the proliferation of computers this would now be relatively easy to do. The list of "essential items" would be determined by the group level administering the "living wage" for a particular area and in addition to food, "essential items', might include utility reticulation, access to water, use of renewable energy or even donations made to charitable organizations.

Basically, the purchase of all "essential items", would generate special receipts that detailed the taxes paid on them. The receipt would be bar-coded to include not only the value, type and date of the transaction, but who the two parties involved were (their unique identification codes), including contact details, their associated sites and bar coded tax numbers.

The special bar coded receipts would act as legal tender, like the old "check/cheque" system, and could be banked or borrowed upon like an insurance policy, but could only be cashed by the person who originally received them or to someone that person endorsed the receipt to, and only used for accredited public services and facilities. This would include any public service or facility run by accredited private enterprise.

Unfortunately, those trying to opt out of capitalism by supporting food and craft markets and other "green" bartering systems would no longer be able to operate outside the new financial system set up by a consensus based government if they wanted to benefit from the "essential item" receipt system.

For GST to be consistently applied, such barter systems would have to generate GST receipts for customers just like all other businesses would. While this might seem an excessive step to close a minor loophole, almost all existing barter systems already utilize the internet, cell phones, credit cards and even bitcoins to conduct their businesses so it is hard to suggest this would be an unreasonable imposition.

The use of a receipt system would allow all individuals and their immediate families, even the poorest ones, to buy use of public services and facilities like higher education, specialist treatment and recreational services of their choice because everyone, even the poorest individuals would be able to pay for them simply by buying food and other "essential items" using their guaranteed "living wage".

As a by-product of the scheme, it would allow the government to check to see if GST was being accurately paid and recorded by everyone involved in business.

Parts of some public services would not be provided through a market-oriented delivery system, however. These include public services that might reduce the sustainability of the environment or require a high level of cooperation among staff, such as police, schoolteachers and medical staff.

The cost of using a resource or of managing activities that involve a resource would be recovered through a Resource Use Tax. This would essentially be an land tax, but it would include more resources, as well as a variable surcharge to compensate the public for the removal of any non-renewable resource or the generation of pollution that occurs on one site but must be cleaned up on another. Land left in it's natural state would not be taxed. Only products grown, raise or made on rural land would be taxed.

Chapter 18:

Sociocracy and Other Similar Paradigm: *describes how a number of governments, businesses, schools and other organizations have already been established using many of the ideas set out in this book. It describes the history of Sociocracy in the Netherlands, and its use particularly in business. It also discusses its parallels with Jose Arizmendiarrietta's work in Mondragon, Spain and the extensive work of Edwin John in helping to set up thousands of similar governing groups in India.*

When I first started to write down my ideas about power and the use of structured consensus decision-making in democratic governments back in the early 1970s, unknown to me a remarkably similar real-life version of it was being developed by a Dutch Engineer named Gerard Endenburg for the operation and management of his large engineering firm.

He had been inspired by the pioneering ideas of his high school teacher Kees Boeke, a Dutch Pacifist Quaker who had established a large school at Bilthoven in 1926 that was run using what he called Sociocratic principles of group decision-making. These principles included making management and curriculum decisions in his school collectively by consensus and doing this in small interlinked groups that included all the students.

The structure also incorporated very basic planning principles. Each group had to set its own goals, work to achieve them and then evaluate their success. He called the small groups "circles" partly because of their looped self-checking, self-correcting design.

Boeke's ideas were based on the social theories of 19th century Philosopher Auguste Comte and later American Sociologist Lester Frank Ward, both of whom had championed the use of scientific logic when dealing with human affairs.

Endenburg refined Boeke's consensus decision-making structure for use in business by removing all religious dogma such as having to love everyone, introducing two way communication between groups, and introducing a way to consider the interests of the market place in their decision-making.

He also clarified the European definition of "consensus" to mean not complete agreement in reaching a decision, but reaching a point where there is no opposition to it, similar to the way consensus has worked in the South Pacific for centuries. He called the method "consent" to distinguish it from what most modern cultures think is consensus.

It proved so successful that Endenburg went on to establish a Sociocracy Consultancy Group (Sociocratisch Centrum) in Rotterdam that today continues to help manage the spread of Sociocracy around the world.

Sociocracy was brought to English speakers by John Buck, an American who went to The Netherlands in the 1980s to learn about Sociocracy and what Endenburg was doing. He proved the efficacy of the system while getting his Master's Degree in Quantitative Sociology and then introduced the ideas to North American organizations looking for an equitable way to include all the views of both management and staff in its decision-making. In 2007 he co-authored a book with Sharon Villines about Sociocracy called "We The People". They updated and republished it in several languages in 2015.

In 2018 Ted Rau and Jerry Koch-Gonzales' book "Many Voices One Song", took any remaining mystery out of Sociocracy by explaining in incredible detail and with many clear examples how literally any one, anywhere could set one up. Ted Rau more recently added to this with his "Who

Decides Who Decides" booklet on getting started in 2021.

Sociocracy is now being used to manage decision-making in an ever growing number of businesses, schools and other for-profit and non-profit organizations across the world.

Today, certified training in Sociocracy is available not only in The Netherlands and the USA but in Canada, Britain, Belgium, Denmark, Germany, Switzerland, France, Spain, Portugal, Brazil, Lithuania, India, Korea, and Australia, among other places.

With mixed support, Sociocracy is now also generating "spin off" decision-making techniques that subtly modify its well tested methodology. Brian Robertson introduced "Holacracy"in 2007, a form of Sociocracy where decision-making groups are intended to be less hierarchical, more autonomous and interlinked together by clearly laid out roles for people to fill rather than job descriptions.

Eight years later, in 2015, James Priest and Bernhard Bockelbrink introduced "Sociocracy 3.0" a variation of Sociocracy which focuses more on clarifying the inter-linked patterns of group governance and making these patterns more easily understood through well organized diagrams and charts.

Technically, the method of consensus decision-making described in this book to form a "Consocracy" is one of them, too. A Consocracy uses virtually all of the principles of Sociocracy in its operation except that it is specifically designed to manage the public governance of millions of people using "structured consensus decision-making". As described earlier, structured consensus decision-making is a method of linking together the public decision-making of thousands of groups on multiple levels to ensure that all of the issues that a public government (of any size) must consider, are taken into account.

§

Twenty years after Kees Boeke set up his school at Bilthoven in The Netherlands, Jose Arizmendiarrietta a young Spanish Priest in the impoverished Basque town of Mondragon started up a new training school in the community to teach the value and methods of working cooperatively.

With his help, some of his students then went on to establish a number of cooperatives in the 1950s and 60s that had many of the same multi-leveled, multi skilled group characteristics that Endenburg's Sociocratic Engineering business later had. Although the Mondragon Cooperatives didn't formally use consensus in their decision-making, they used something similar called "equilibrio", or "balance", a uniquely Basque concept of inclusion, to reach group decisions.

By the mid 1980s, they had developed a complex multi-leveled cooperative structure which in addition to involving more than 100 industrial, agricultural and housing cooperatives, also included 46 cooperatively run schools and training centers with 35,000 students, 270 retail stores, a cooperative bank with 180 branch offices as well as cooperative health care and social support services for all its members.

§

Many of the decision-making ideas that Dutch Sociocracy and the Mondragon Cooperatives embraced also spontaneously started up in India around the same time. Coincidentally, it was a young Catholic Priest that led this endeavor as well.

Edwin John was appointed as a parish priest in a village in the State of Tamalnadu on the southeast tip of India in 1970. It was a very poor area with a high crime rate, and to try to deal with it he organized the villages into neighborhood groups of around 30 families each to talk about their problems and cooperatively work on ways to overcome them.

To stop anyone from dominating the group, everyone had to sit in a single circle facing each other and talk without any sound amplification. In the beginning, group decisions were not made by consensus (Sociocratic consent) but there was an effort to seek some degree of "convergence" or common ground before any action was taken.

Because of the large population, he organized the groups into a hierarchy of decision-making where one representative member from each neighborhood group came together with other neighborhood representatives on a second level to fix larger problems of mutual interest. More layers were added as the areas of interest and numbers of people involved grew.

This "bottom-up" hierarchical structure became a way of setting up a housing society, a savings society, and a village court system, and the ideas eventually spread to all of India's Catholic Church parishes involving many thousands of village groups.

It was an attractive method of organizing people because at the lowest and most important level where final decisions were ultimately carried out, the groups were small enough for each person involved to feel valued. When changes came they knew they had played a part in making them happen. In less than 6 years the crime rate in the villages dropped to almost zero.

The success of Edwin John's approach to local problem solving caught the attention of the State Government of Kerala. They saw it could be a way to help reduce poverty in local neighborhoods and villages as it empowered women to control their own future. Many women in India, particularly poor women, had become virtually powerless in the Country's male dominated society, but this system offered women direct access to finance, to other sympathetic women and to other resources that could help them find a way forward.

The State Government in 1998 rebranded Edwin John's model as "Kudumbashree" and focused its attention specifically on helping poor women.

The system proved to be incredibly successful. It also proved to be a very effective way for the Indian Government and other institutions to ensure their own "self-help" initiatives reached back down to those in small neighborhoods and villages where they were needed. Kudumbashree has now been adopted by the Government of India's Ministry of Rural Development as part of its nation wide poverty eradication program.

When a fourth level of women's Kudumbashree was established, however, the politicians in government started to get nervous. They realized the system could ultimately become more powerful than they were so they passed laws to limit Kudumbashree groups to 3 levels.

The new laws have given local politicians (mainly male) some breathing space, but it has not stopped women from asserting themselves in local politics. While the national government has been trying for some time with little success to achieve sexual parity in local elections, in some of the areas where Kudumbashree exist today, women now out-number men in local government.

More recently, Edwin John has turned his attention to helping set up "Children's Parliaments" based on the premise that the future of the planet is in the hands of our children. The concerns of Children's Parliaments include many of the same issues that the United Nations Sustainable Development Goals deal with, such as poverty, crime, health, housing, education, finance, clean water, and global warming among others.

He has found that young adults can be very resourceful and can often resolve local problems by themselves or by focusing sufficient attention on them to gain the support of parents, friends, and local politicians.

Edwin John is now also introducing Sociocratic consensus based decision-making into the Children's Parliaments to better insure that all people in each group are given equal recognition. It is something he has always strived for, but Sociocratic methodology helps to ensure this.

With the more recent help of the United Nations, there are now many thousands of multi-level neighborhood groups across India, Africa, Asia, the Americas and Europe.

The neighborhood groups are a growing force on the planet for they are reintroducing community values, trust and understanding into a world where for various reasons these important social attributes have been slowly disappearing.

§

The twentieth century saw the development of many other consensus based approaches to public group decision-making as well. In the 1930s and 40s Alex F Osborn developed his theories on "Brainstorming", which contained a number of ideas later picked up by other group decision-making methodologies.

His ideas included consciously trying to involve everyone in small group discussions, judging new ideas by their value to the group not by the status of the person suggesting them, taking time to adequately assess every idea, and using a systematic approach to reaching conclusions. He also supported the use of an independent person leading the process, involving people with the widest possible range of opinions, and initially sharing ideas anonymously.

In the 1950s Olaf Helmer and Norman Dalkey of the Rand Corporation developed the "Delphi Technique" discussed in Chapter 5, which focused on the anonymous multiple exchanges of information between people with very different knowledge, skills, and experience to reach common ground.

In the 1970s a group of American hippies produced a series of articles outlining how to make decisions using consensus. The articles were pulled together in 1981 in a book called "Building United Judgment". It is often described as the "go to" book on the subject as it was very detailed on how to resolve differences among group members, handle emotions, use group facilitators, and proceed when common agreement could not be reached.

Also in the 1970's Dr. John Rohrbaugh began his development of "Value Knowledge Management" using computers to help diverse groups reach consensus on complex issues. By pure chance, my wife and I met John while he was still working on his doctorate when we took a job as house parents of a group home for juvenile delinquents following our African adventures. We had taken the job to give me time to write about the hidden problems of democratic paternalism and the downside of power, and he and his wife were one of the relieving couples for us on weekends.

For his doctorate, John was perfecting a way to help local politicians make some very controversial decisions. He was working with a computer program that could accurately predict what land parcels local politicians might consider for public purchase to create a greenbelt around the university town of Boulder Colorado when various parcels came up for sale. The analytical method took into simultaneous consideration the expressed values and interests of each politician, and it was so efficient that, rather than having to spend hours debating the merits of each land parcel, the politicians largely ended up relying on the computer to make their decisions transparent and more accountable to the town.

My writing was interrupted by a job offer in Zambia and I lost touch with the couple, but a few years ago I found them again through the internet. Not surprisingly, Dr Rohrbaugh's research four decades on had become considerably more sophisticated. He was well past finding majority solutions to problems and was then seriously engaged in developing tools that sought consensus among multiple factions with multiple conflicting values. "Value Knowledge Management" as he described his approach, considered not only information that could be gleaned from known sources, such as personal interest surveys and data files, but those within each individual that were unspoken and unnamed.

When multiple factions with conflicting values needed to solve a problem, his approach was to work first with each faction separately to clarify their real interests. Once clarified, he could then calculate a solution that jointly maximized each faction's interests. In a joint meeting, all involved were then given the results and presented with the task of finding an even better solution. This approach meant that everyone in the group was not bargaining toward an unknown solution but bargaining away from a known one. This considerably improved the chances of a successful outcome.

More recently a number of less complex computer based tools have been developed as well. None of them consider the use of consensus or Sociocratic consent decision-making in the way Dr Rohrbaugh's program does, but most try to handle complex space-time questions and the chaos of generating new ideas that might identify better, more mutually acceptable outcomes.

One of the earliest computer programs to do this that was easily accessible to the public was Microsoft's Windows based "Project" program introduced in 1990. Users started by listing all the tasks that needed to be done to achieve a particular goal and both the time and materials that would be needed to complete each task. The program then produced a time-line diagram that pictorially showed how the goal could be achieved.

Among other things the program identified critical points that could disrupt or even stop a goal from being achieved if certain things did not happen first.

A number of other publically accessible programs came out after that which tried to simplify or improve many of the things Microsoft's Project could do. Today there are literally dozens of brainstorming, mind mapping and/or project timing programs that use various methods to help people think laterally or vertically, link actions together and/or prioritize actions by time, cost or importance.

One program introduced in 2012 that sits apart from most of the newer ones is Ben Knight and Richard Bartlett's "Loomio" program. It attempts to seek consensus on a project or action among all those involved.

It starts like the others by setting the goal of the project or action and then getting everyone involved to "brainstorm" ways it might be achieved. This can be done anonymously if desired. But then it shows in pie diagrams the collective responses to each of the ideas by percentage of the overall group that agrees, disagrees, abstains or wants to throw out (veto) the idea altogether. All those involved are then encouraged to suggest modifications to any of the ideas put forward until consensus is reached on one of them.

Like the idea of Children's Parliaments, it too is now beginning to spread around the world as a viable way to find solutions to problems that are supported by more than just half those involved.

So it turns out that the 50 year process I've gone through to come up with a form of government that might actually fix the planet, only confirms the conclusions already reached by many others working independently on the problems. It is not a big leap then, to suggest that there might be some merit in the ideas, the methodology and the structure of the proposed planetary fix discussed so far.

Chapter 19

A Way Out of this Mess: *describes how an updated version of democracy using a "structured" version of consensus decision-making could be introduced over time to any sized group of people, anywhere, in just 5 steps. The first step would involve people trying out consensus decision making in their own club meetings, family outings and other non-threatening decision-making situations just to see how much less divisive it is. The last step would be voluntarily adopting the "Consocratice Plan" as an upgrade or amendment to an existing government's constitution or a corporation's management procedures.*

Three things seemed clear to me back in 1972 when I first realised that most of our democratic institutions contained several serious flaws in them. One was that any attempt to fix them would need to take into account the intense, complex, ever changing chaos that we all have to live with on this planet. There is no reason to think that new life-changing ideas, inventions and problems would not continue to emerge as we all go through indefinable time.

However, chaos is not as random as the name implies. Mathematicians and other experts on the subject have shown that over time, discernable, often repetitive patterns will eventually appear in chaotic events. The significance of any chaos is formed at its very beginning. If any pattern is generated by chaos, that pattern is actually set by the very first steps that occur seemingly randomly.

The Consocratic Plan contained in this book has focused on setting up that beginning event for precisely this reason. Even with a clear set of goals, principles, rights, responsibilities and rules, that is, with a much more detailed constitution, the ultimate form of any democratic government that considers the rights and needs of everyone on an equal basis in a sustainable environment and well functioning market economy will be almost impossible to predict.

The second thing that has been clear to me from the beginning is that the tools that our governments use to handle the chaos must, by necessity, end up as fractals; that is, be in a form that looks and acts the same way on many different levels of government. Public understanding of how governments work is absolutely essential if people are to support and participate in them.

The third is that any serious update of an existing democratic government must be introduced through the efforts of many small groups of people rather than through the efforts of either just one person or an entire country.

I had thought that change from either the top or bottom almost always required force, and one critical prerequisite I had set myself from the very beginning was that a democratic solution to the planet's existing problems could not be achieved through violence, terrorism or war.

I have since discovered, thankfully, that my third concern may not have been entirely warranted. The very nature of consensus decision-making seems to generate peace and social tolerance among people rather than violence, terrorism or war.

Nevertheless, I have set out the following suggestions on how to fix the mess we're in on this planet by beginning with what small groups of people might do to start the process. Even if a Consocracy is established by one of the other two methods, the final step in all three approaches would be the same.

§

I know the likelihood of any government updating its laws to use consensus is extremely remote. If there was a quick fix to the problems we face we'd have found it by now. Certainly the five hundred sixty individually approached publishers and agents who "passed" on this book despite specifically professing to be interested in Political Science did not believe in the possibility. Not even one bothered to read the full manuscript.

—

Their reluctance, I suspect, was at least partly because consensus decision-making is now a lost art among most communities on this planet. Even the best democracies today resolve problems by identifying two (or more) solutions and then forcing voters or their representatives to choose just one of them.

This unavoidably forces everyone to take sides. The process splits communities and creates winners and losers, which is often followed by a feeling of alienation and anger among those who lose out.

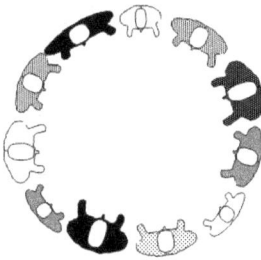

Decisions by Consensus   Decisions by the Majority

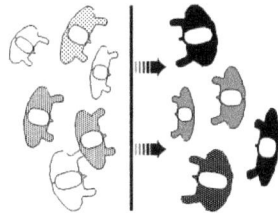

It is for this reason I believe that the single most important 1st step any of us might take to update our democracies and our chances of survival on this planet is to try to convince the people we live with, the people we work with, the people in any existing local group we are involved in to "Think Globally, Act Locally;" that is, to make their decisions by the consensus of everyone in that group rather than by a vote of the majority.

Examples:
- A family deciding where to go on vacation,
- Teenagers choosing the location of their next social gathering,
- A neighborhood group setting the theme for their annual street party,
- A sports club committee deciding who should be their next president,
- A community service club deciding what project to support,

- A town centre Chamber of Commerce setting the year's business support program,
- A university political science class deciding with their teacher what they will focus their studies on.
- A local government town planning committee deciding what developments to approve.

The motivation for a group to change its method of decision-making might be the noble desire of members to end paternalism and give everyone in the group equal power to make decisions. It might be the desire to bring a divided group, club or committee back together, or it might simply be the gentle push of someone who believes in the idea. In any event, the experiment would not require the group to change anything else.

Group, club or committee members would still be elected, appointed or volunteer as previously. No existing laws would need to change. Nothing would have to change other than that all group members would have to agree to talk through their differences and reach decisions without opposition. Remember, as used by "primitive" societies, consensus does not mean 100% agreement. It means there is no disagreement. The difference may sound like meaningless semantics but it is extremely significant. It means that all anger, hate and divisiveness have been removed from the outcome.

While reaching consensus in a group, club or committee might seem an improbable first step, there are actually a number of groups, committees, and even a few governments around this planet already leading the way. For instance almost all indigenous communities in the South Pacific make their local decisions by consensus. In addition, the British Guernsey Islands off the coast of France are now largely run by a series of committees that use consensus.

There are also two Canadian districts, the Northwest Territories and Nunavut Province that reach their decisions in part by consensus. More relevant to larger communities and governments, most of the 100 or so "Green" or environmental political parties around the world, many of which now have elected representatives in government, have used consensus to set their policies since the 1980s, and as pointed out earlier, most jury trials and Quaker meetings have used consensus decision-making for centuries.

To ensure some likelihood of success in replacing majority vote decision-making with consensus decision-making, any group or committee attempting to use consensus will probably need to be very small initially. It is much easier to understand the views of 10 or 15 people in depth than it is to get to know intimately the hopes and desires of 50 people.

Reaching consensus in small groups is not impossible, for even today most democracies do it every time they vote on anything. This may sound surprising, but every time a decision is made by majority vote, everyone on the majority side must reach consensus among themselves on the details of what they are actually voting to support. In a city council with 15 members, for instance, at least 8 members must reach mutual agreement on exactly what they are choosing to do. While there is likely to be less diversity of thought in half a group, some diversity, even among the majority half is usually unavoidable. So in reality, even majority vote decision-making often requires reaching consensus among a group of people.

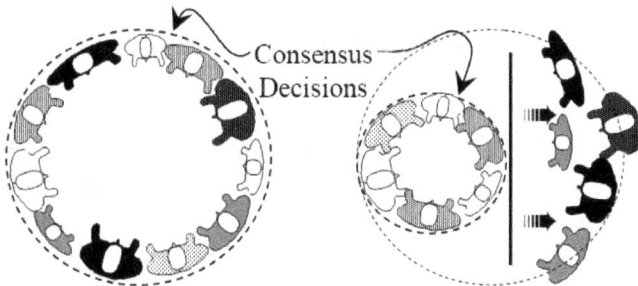

Decisions by Consensus   Decisions by the Majority

While most groups of people on the majority side don't actually vote among themselves when they decide what they will support in a full democratic vote, some do. In such circumstances, it means that only a majority of the majority, or as little as 26% of the people in that democracy are actually making decisions for the public. It means that the "majority" of people are not really running that government at all, not by any stretch of the imagination.

Just the change to consensus decision-making by a club or committee would create a fundamental shift in the group's approach to problem solving. Everyone knows how our current democratic decision-making works. In parts of the world it has been practiced for centuries. An idea is raised, its good and bad points are debated, and then it is voted upon. If more than half agree with it, the idea becomes applicable to everyone.

Unfortunately, today almost no one knows how consensus works. Most people only know that it's impossible to use in large groups and it can be hijacked by narcissists. In most of the world, knowledge of the art, value and practice of consensus decision-making has been lost for generations. In our modern world, few have ever had the chance to discover that decisions made by consensus are usually more holistic than majority vote decisions; that they unite communities rather than divide them; and that they are often cheaper and quicker to implement in the long run because they can be carried out immediately without the ongoing hassle of opponents trying to change the decision or stop its implementation.

Complicating this lack of knowledge, in current political debate the usual reaction of a person in the majority group to an idea not in sympathy with one's own, is to rubbish it. It is a response that has been taught over centuries of democratic contest, and it is a response that some will find difficult to give up.

For these reasons, any group, club or committee that does decide to change its majority vote decision-making to consensus decision-making will probably need to adopt some initial informal rules of conduct to help all members stay focused on the committee or group's usual tasks.

In most committees today, for instance, the chairperson's primary role is to keep order and ensure democratic processes are followed. In many committees, he or she does not even vote unless there is a tie and a "casting vote" is required.

A slightly revised role for the chairperson in a group using consensus might be for the chairperson to act as a neutral mediator to reduce tensions in heated debates, similar to the way a Samoan Orator manages a community meeting. The chairperson could also be the facilitator in identifying similarities between different ideas in search of a solution acceptable to all.

The chairperson might even be the person who is given responsibility for deciding what to do if consensus cannot be reached. For instance, he or she might be given by the others in the group, the power to invoke a previously agreed alternative means of decision-making in such circumstances, such as "consensus, less one".

In a fully operating Consocracy, there are better options when this happens, but in the early stages of setting one up, when consensus cannot be reached, a back up plan for the group's decision-making is a very good idea.

§

The reason why decisions will take more time in the early stages of consensus decisions-making, is because every member of a group must get to know intimately every other member of the group. It is not enough just to know every member's name. Each member must become sufficiently familiar with everyone else in the group to know their families, where they live, what their hobbies are and why they want to be a representative.

In a fully functioning Consocracy, it is a fundamental requirement that every group's representative must provide such information in writing and keep it up to date as part of the representative's public record.

Getting to know the other members in a group well can be shortened with the help of computers and the internet. Facebook, Twitter, Skype, WhatSapp, Zoom, FaceTime and other social networking tools used outside formal gatherings of the group are powerful methods of communication that can rapidly speed up understanding between people. Other computer aids worth considering include programs like BrainStorm, Loomio and Weaver, which facilitate the exchange of ideas, assist in problem structuring, and support decision-making processes.

Possibly the most powerful way that computers can help

very diverse groups of people find mutually agreeable solutions to complex problems, however, is to use them to identify what a mutually agreeable consensus decision might look like. Dr. John Rohrbaugh's "Value Knowledge Management" computer program, for instance, can help such groups reach consensus by considering the values and interests of each person involved individually. By using a computer, group members can then begin their discussions from a known possible solution rather than try to blindly create one from scratch. This considerably improves the chances of a successful outcome.

§

I believe the successful use of consensus by a number of small local groups, clubs or committees will, in time, encourage local governments to try it too, and that would be a very significant 2nd step in introducing it to central or national government decision-making. This is because local governments have the legal right to affect the lives of many people through the powers they enjoy.

What they can legally make decisions on, of course, varies from community to community and from country to country depending on existing empowering legislation, but in most cases the governments of towns and cities can regulate private land use as well as collect taxes to pay for local public improvements like roads, parks, libraries, water supply, sewage treatment and other public services and facilities. Both are very powerful local democratic decision-making functions.

Like the 1st step, this would not require any changes to existing laws. I have not found any democratic government anywhere whose constitution prohibits its representatives from making their decisions by consensus.

All members of a local council would still have to be elected by the public in their usual way, but at that point they could then voluntarily agree among themselves to use consensus to make their council decisions. Using consensus would instantly change the outlook and image of a local government to the people it governed. This 2nd step in the adoption of a consensus based central or national government would inspire public cooperation and community spirit and it would encourage other communities to follow their example.

§

The 3rd step in setting up a consensus based national government would be to set up a method for local residents to become voluntary community advisors to local government to provide elected members with detailed knowledge of local activities. This too, would not require any law change.

Today, most local governments include not only elected representatives but non-elected advisors to help representatives make their decisions and to carry out the decisions local governments make. The advisors typically include experts like administrators, engineers, economists and planners, but there is usually no formal criteria or procedure that local governments must follow to select them, so some could be selected as "community advisors" by using a simple, informal version of "structured consensus decision-making". As described elsewhere, this is a multi-level method of choosing representatives by consensus.

The reason why this would be helpful is that most local governments have grown so large that elected representatives rarely know much about the inner workings of most neighborhood residential, commercial or industrial areas they represent or the lives of the people in them. Similarly, few local residents today have any understanding of what local governments actually do, much less how or why. The introduction of voluntary community advisors to councils would greatly reduce such ignorance.

At this early stage the use of structured consensus decision-making methodology to select the community advisers would not have to consider all the matters a full consensus based government or Consocracy might consider, but such a multi-leveled method for selecting them would encourage local residents throughout the jurisdiction of the local government to support and peacefully work together with their political leaders. The advisor positions and method of choosing them could be entirely voluntary and need not cost the local government anything.

The population of the area being governed would determine the number of "levels" needed for its volunteer community advisors. An urban/rural area with under 50,000 people might need only two or three levels of community advisors. If there were a million people involved, there might need to be four or five levels.

Once it became clear that "structured consensus decision-making" works to introduce community advisors into local government decision-making, it might then be possible to take the 4th step by widening the role of the volunteer local multi-leveled community advisors into other decision-making groups operating within the local government's jurisdiction. Initially, the most logical "community advisor" responsibilities might involve only land use management matters like helping council members decide the location of new housing or commercial buildings. However, the local parent-teachers group or school board in a town might consider it helpful to develop a close relationship with a local community advisor too since he or she would probably be involved in helping local governments determine where schools are built and how they might be expanded.

In time, other levels of government involved in public education, roading, health care, public utilities and community services might find it helpful and economically beneficial to add the council's voluntary community advisors to their own meetings to help them coordinate their activities. Such cooperation would help regional hospitals work with regional transport systems and higher education providers to ensure their accessibility to all those who need to use or staff them.

This is actually a more important part of the 4th step in the upgrade of a democratic government than it might seem, as the ultimate form of a Consocracy pulls together all forms of public decision-making into a single body at every level of government, and this 4th voluntary step would demonstrate how such a major change in political decision-making might work.

Under a fully operating Consocracy, local governments on each level would not only administer land use, but oversee public education, public health, justice and police services as well, with the assistance of sub-committees focused on these areas. The political responsibilities at each level would be much more explicit than they are now and would depend on the size of the geographical area and number of people they represented, but all government decisions would then be able to be much more holistic than they are now, as each of their decisions would have to consider all 5 types of systems of change previously discussed at once, i.e. personal, economic, equity, community and environmental change.

Up to this point, no laws would have to change. Local government decision-making by consensus would be voluntary and the establishment of community advisors would not require any new legislation.

§

However, the final step, Step 5, would unavoidably require updating existing laws. This last step would involve updating an existing democratic government's constitution using part or all of the components set out in the Consocratic Plan, the final (20th) Chapter of the "Power, Chaos or Consensus?" book. This step would require a "leap of faith" in the Consocratic form of government, and would probably only work once the general pubic of a whole country had become familiar and comfortable with how well and peaceful consensus based decision-making worked after successfully following the first 4 steps.

Given the major law changes that would have to be made by a whole country taking the 5th step, small island nations like the Virgin Islands, the Cayman Islands, the Isle of Man, or Bermuda might seem the most likely candidates to make such a change. Unfortunately, however, most island nations are tax havens heavily reliant on handling the wealth of international corporations in secret. They could not easily afford to make, much less lead, such a change.

More likely, any major attempt to set up a structured consensus based central government would probably have to be led by a small country with more diversified interests. Some countries, such as The Netherlands, Denmark, Norway, Sweden, Switzerland, Australia and New Zealand already have a history of social reform that might facilitate the introduction of structured consensus decision-making.

The final step could be taken simply by formally adopting the full Consocratic Plan included in Chapter 20 of the original "Power, Chaos or Consensus?" book as an adjunct or replacement to an existing nation's constitution, or in some cases like New Zealand's, as its first comprehensive constitution.

The full Consocratic Plan essentially has 8 Parts, which are:

Part 1. Plan Commencement
Part 2. The 5 Principles of a Consensus Based Democratic Government
Part 3. The 12 Goals of Humanity
Part 4. The Rights and Responsibilities of both Individuals and Groups
    a. Involving Personal Systems of change
    b. Involving Economic Systems of change
    c. Involving Equity Systems of change
    d. Involving Community Systems of change
    e. Involving Environmental Systems of change
Part 5. Fundamental Rules
Part 6. Recommended Rules
Part 7. Termination
Part 8. Interpretation of Key Words

The constitutional update would not have to happen all at once. It could happen in several stages. For instance, under the rules in Part 5, it is essential to assign a globally unique identification number to every individual and to associate all individuals with a publicly recorded, globally unique "site".

Both might best occur prior to any constitutional update. It is possible that this requirement might be opposed by some human rights advocates despite the substantial increase in individual rights that adoption of the Consocratic Plan would allow. The more time that is given to help people understand why they should be given a globally unique identification number and be associated with a single site, the more likely everyone will accept their introduction.

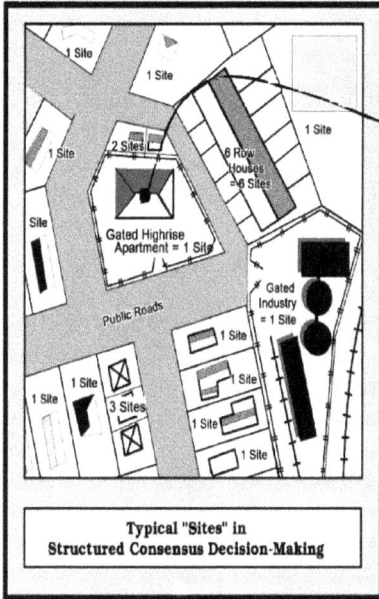

Typical "Sites" in
Structured Consensus Decision-Making

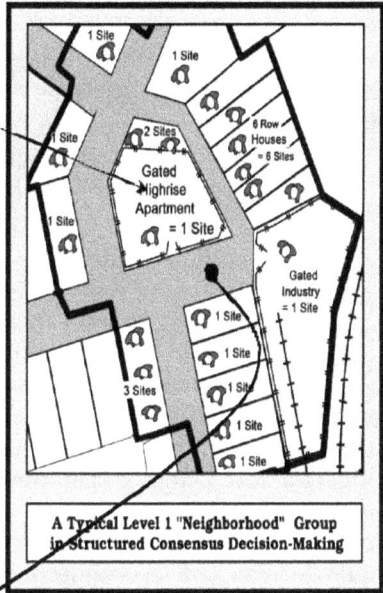

A Typical Level 1 "Neighborhood" Group
in Structured Consensus Decision-Making

A Typical Level 2 "Village" Group with
Representatives from 8 Neighborhood Groups

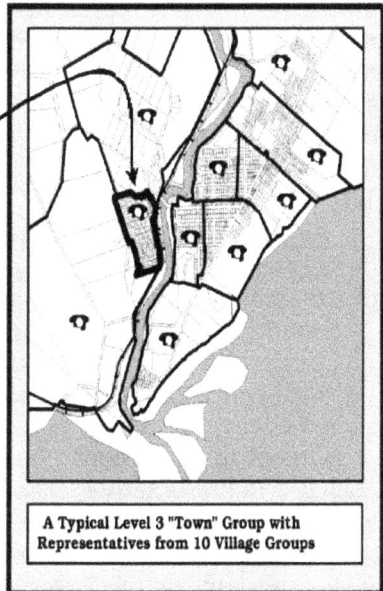

A Typical Level 3 "Town" Group with
Representatives from 10 Village Groups

Public discussion of some parts of the new constitution might actually best occur some time after most of the new constitution is adopted. In particular, Part 6 involves suggested tax and monetary changes which are not essential to the operation of a Consocracy so could be added at a later date.

Also, a number of the Rights and Responsibilities included in Part 4, namely those "recommended" and those "possible", are not essential to the operation of a Consocracy. These could also be left out initially until there was an opportunity for everyone to consider them in detail.

The four diagrams on the previous page illustrate how the first three levels of "Structured Consensus Decision-Making Groups are formed, starting with what constitutes a "Site", then what "Neighborhood","Village" and "Town" levels might look like.

The last diagram on the right schematically shows the organizational similarity of the various levels of decision-making groups. Every black circle in the diagram is a decision-making group of representatives.

The size of the circle identifies the number of people (and number of sites) it represents; the larger the circle, the more people (and sites) represented. Each black circle or decision-making group is set out and operated in the same way as every other black circle or group. The large black circle in the middle of the diagram is simply a detailed look at one of the decision-making groups on level 3. All groups on all levels actually look and operate like this.

As shown in the large detailed black circle in the middle of the diagram on the following page every circle or group is split into 6 sections. Five of the sections are labeled "Personal", "Economic", "Equity", "Community" and "Environmental", (PEECE) for the 5 types of systems each group decision must consider, and each of these sections contains two shaded and labeled ovals.

One of the 6 sections of each black circle or group is only labeled "Representative". This person provides the "link" between that group and a group on the next level of government, but takes no direct responsibly for any of the 5 types of systems on the lower level.

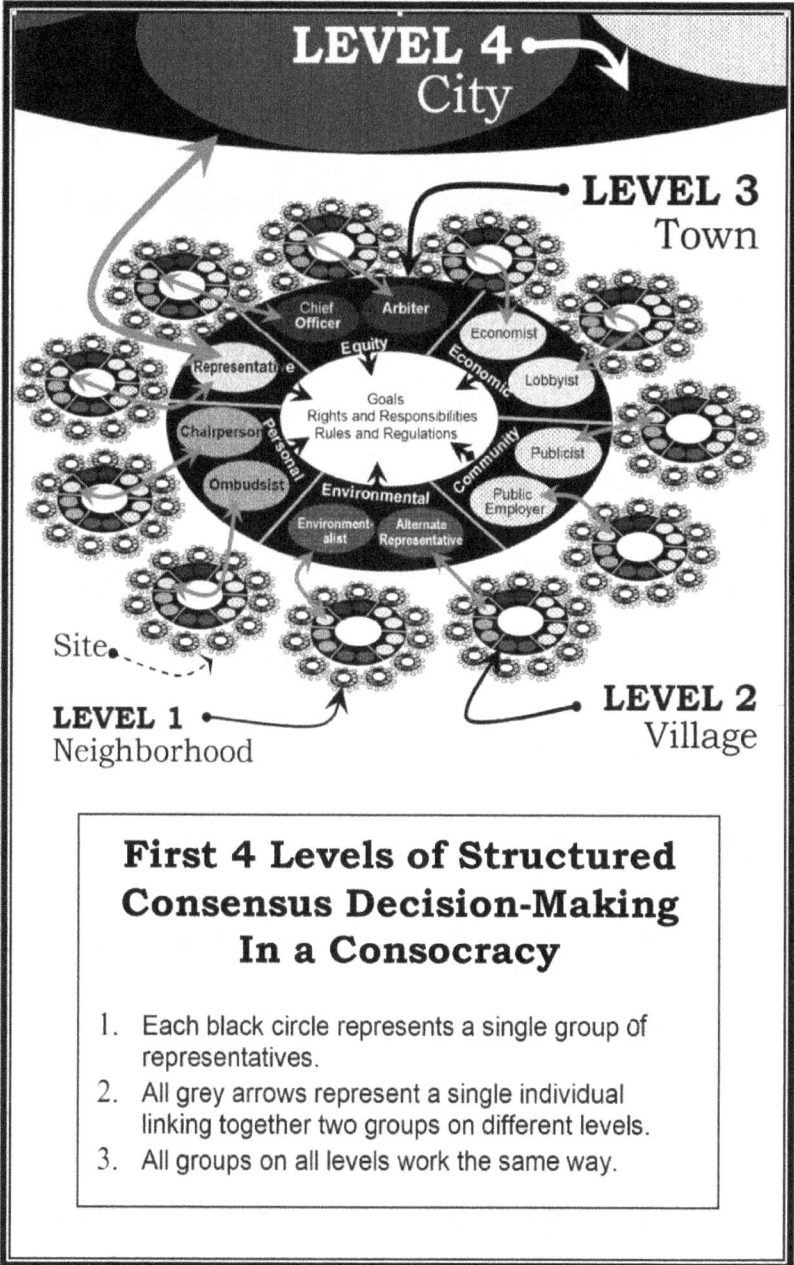

LEVEL 4
City

LEVEL 3
Town

Chief Officer

Arbiter

Economist

Equity

Representative

Economic

Lobbyist

Goals
Rights and Responsibilities
Rules and Regulations

Chairperson

Personal

Community

Publicist

Ombudsist

Environmental

Public Employer

Environment-alist

Alternate Representative

Site

LEVEL 1
Neighborhood

LEVEL 2
Village

First 4 Levels of Structured Consensus Decision-Making In a Consocracy

1. Each black circle represents a single group of representatives.
2. All grey arrows represent a single individual linking together two groups on different levels.
3. All groups on all levels work the same way.

The thin grey arrows represent the link that the same individual provides between two groups on two different levels.

Every member in a group other than the group's representative must take on one of the ministerial or cabinet roles, which are the variously shaded ovals within the black circles. For groups with less than 11 members some of these roles must be doubled up. For instance the member responsible for economic systems in a group with less than 11 members may have to take on both the Economist and the Lobbyist roles. For groups larger than 11 members, cabinet or ministerial roles should be shared.

What is most important is that at least one group member responsible for each of the 5 types of systems, as well as the representative linked to the upper level group must all be present and involved in every decision made by that group.

For this reason all groups must contain a minimum of 6 representatives, as shown by the 6 short arrows into the centre of the black circle which link the decisions of every member to the goals, principles, rights, responsibilities, rules and regulations applicable to that group. Preferably, groups should not contain more than 30 members so that all representatives may sit together in a single circle and easily talk with each other face to face, although up to 42 members are permissible in exceptional circumstances.

Chapter 20: (Not included)

The Consocratic Plan: is a complete set of Goals, Principles, Rights, Responsibilities and Rules, that any sized group of people could voluntarily adopt over time to progressively and peacefully update local, regional and national democratic governments (and other institutions and businesses) without breaking any existing civil laws and procedures, and without having to resort to violence, terrorism or war.

About the Author:
Ted Wells

Ted was born and raised near Boston, Massachusetts and educated as an Architect and Urban Designer in Oregon and Colorado. After completing his degree in the sixties, he chose to join the Peace Corps in Ethiopia rather than the war in Vietnam.

For three years he planned new towns in very remote parts of the Rift Valley while his wife, Helen, treated sick people and cattle there. They then spent a year travelling the back roads of Europe in a VW van exploring their new towns to see what he should have done in Africa. Eventually they returned to the United States where he worked for 5 years as a planner for a small city in Colorado.

In the mid-1970s, he and his wife became disillusioned with American politics so they moved their young family to New Zealand in search of an alternative approach to peace, social justice and the environment. They found a comfortable home and welcoming community by the Tasman Sea and decided to stay.

As a dual US-New Zealand citizen, his professional planning career has taken him around the globe many times writing, studying and/or designing plans for governments, NGOs and businesses across the USA, Canada, the Caribbean, Great Britain, Europe, North Africa, China, Korea, Japan, Malaysia and the South pacific.

He has written plans for several US communities, the World Bank, the Japanese Aid Agency, a Gold Mine, the Sultan of Brunei, the Emperor of Ethiopia and for dozens of city, regional and national governments around the Pacific Rim including New Zealand, Australia, Samoa and Papua New Guinea. He has also been on the New Zealand Planning Institute's Governing Board of Directors, written articles for several journals and helped win for BECA Consultants, his employer for much of this time, several professional planning awards.

Both his books, "Power, Chaos or Consensus?" and "The Old Man in the Bag" are about some of his professional and personal travels and the ideas he has come across working on the edge of political decision-making in various parts of the world, which have given him hope there could be a better future for us.

It was in Ethiopia where Ted first learned that even selfless good intentions don't always leave those being "helped" with smiles on their faces; that life decisions are rarely ever black and white even though most of our public institutions currently force us to solve problems by first polarizing their possible solutions.

However, it was not until he spent two years in Samoa four decades later that he finally understood just how there might be another way through the current global mess we now find ourselves in. It was there helping local communities prepare coastal management plans against sea level rise due to global warming that he realised their centuries old consensus decision-making methods held the solution.

www.ingramcontent.com/pod-product-compliance
Lightning Source LLC
Chambersburg PA
CBHW050123280326
41933CB00010B/1227